F-BOMB

Longevity Made Easy

Julia Jones, PhD
aka Dr Rock

F-BOMB

CONTENTS

PART ONE

F*cked
Why it all Failed

4

PART TWO

Future
How to make it F'ing Fabulous

PART THREE

Faster
Habit Tracker

Acknowledgements

Thank you to the many family members, friends, colleagues, and clients who have been on this journey with me over the past few years of researching and writing this health trilogy book series. In addition, there are many people in this field who have inspired me and continued to keep me motivated in this lifelong quest to discover the easiest route to a long, healthy life. I hope you enjoy the read and that the insights featured in this book help you transform your wellness in the way they transformed mine.

Disclaimer

The content within this book is not to be considered as medical recommendations. It is educational information that according to published research is likely to help you reduce your risk of chronic disease and increase your expected healthy life expectancy.

As with any health-related activity, you should first consult with your doctor if you believe you may have any underlying health concerns that make some of these techniques inappropriate for you.

FOREWORD

by Steph McGovern

I meet a lot of guests on my TV show but interviewing Julia about her Neuron book and smart wellness programme in 2021 made an instant impact on me. What she was saying about the habit-based approach to health seemed so easy. It was exactly what I was looking for to fix my own long-term health struggles. I gave her my contact details as she was leaving the studio and asked if I could do her 8-week programme. That meeting not only transformed my health, it also transformed my life because my life was hampered by my ongoing health issues that had become my new normal. Julia's 8-week smart wellness course was fascinating and showed me how to make the simple habit adjustments that put me on a new path. I learnt so much. This new knowledge was hugely empowering. After enduring a lifetime of gut-related health problems I was finally in control of my body. Within a few months I felt fantastic, and still do. This is now my new normal.

I believed in Julia's work so much that I invested in her business. Together we want to communicate these simple principles to as many people as possible so they can benefit from this smart wellness approach in the way we have. This final book in Julia's health trilogy makes it even simpler to understand why, and how, to adopt this smart wellness approach.

INTRODUCTION

Let's just say the past year has been a game of two halves. My '*Neuron: Smart Wellness Made Easy*' book entered the Amazon Bestseller list after I got some national media coverage and appeared on Steph's Channel 4 TV show. Lots of great things started happening after that. Progress was being made.

The smart wellness programme in my Neuron book was turned into a virtual, on-demand programme being offered to workforces by leading corporate employers.

Embedding the smart wellness plan in my own daily routine had extended my healthy life expectancy by 23 years in just 23 months. I knew these smart wellness habits worked, not just for me, but also for other clients who successfully embraced them.

My start-up company seemed to be surviving the pandemic.

Life was great.

Then an unexpected snafu blew up in my personal life. It had a significant negative impact on my mental and physical health. However, these things happen. The research for this book was well underway when all that emotional and financial drama erupted. I decided to immerse myself even deeper in it. Partly to simply help distract me from all the stress that I was dealing with. What I discovered was a tonne of incredible research that I hadn't properly dug into before. This longevity field is moving so fast.

In this final book in my Health Trilogy, I'm going to introduce you to some ground-breaking concepts, and some key cellular pathways called AMPK, mTOR and the sirtuins that are now thought to be our key to achieving longevity. I call them our three amigos. You're going to hear a lot about them in the coming years as this knowledge enters the mainstream. I'm also going to show you how we got into this fricking health mess in the first place. We'll chart 6 million years of things that we now know played a role in our health downfall. I'll also talk about the reasons why some people successfully adopted the smart wellness plan presented in my Neuron book, and some did not.

I hope that by reading this book you'll feel fully up-to-speed with the new knowledge relating to health and longevity and will decide to start adopting these smart wellness habits in your own daily routine, if you haven't yet done so. I want you to know our lives and daily habits have consequences. My relationship break-up sent my heart rate variability and gut diversity plummeting downwards, as you can see in the following charts from my data. It's taken me almost a year to get back to where I was. But what I really noticed during this personally turbulent episode is that my new smart wellness habits stayed pretty consistent. There was an initial wobble and the inevitable leaning towards wine and junk food which impacted my measurements. But essentially my new routine stayed intact and eventually pulled me back on course.

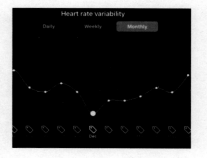 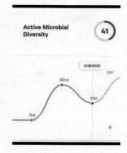

The chart on the left shows the negative effects of that prolonged period of chronic stress on my heart rate variability. In January, I finally managed to retain ownership of my home and the stress gradually reduced from that point on. You can see how my HRV scores gradually recovered from that point and are now back up to my original baseline.

As you can see in the chart on the right, my gut diversity was wiped out by a course of antibiotics for a tooth infection in 2020. It dropped to 3% diversity. I successfully built it back up to 82% in 2021 through my smart wellness habit routine, fasting and diverse plant-dominated eating habits. The chronic stress during that subsequent period negatively impacted it again and knocked it back down to 41%. I'm gradually rebuilding it.

Don't underestimate the impact of stress on your gut microbiome and general underlying physiology and neurobiology. The gut and brain are connected via a two-way communication channel (the gut-brain-axis). This experience has been a true test of the resilience of my habits. They didn't let me down. They are my new normal.

1

F*ck!

What's going on?

I've called this final book in my Health Trilogy "F-Bomb" for two reasons.

1. As I dug deep into the research over the past few years, I began noticing that F-words were popping up freakishly often. So, I began collecting them. They will narrate our 6 million+ year health journey, and our quest for longevity, throughout the following chapters.

2. The more I read, the more shocked I became at how wrong we've been. The health sector is on the verge of a monumental disruption that will change how we view modern medicine and wellness forever. F*ck is the word that sums it up rather effectively and it's something I've uttered regularly throughout my research whenever I stumbled on new science that suggested staggering findings. It's also the word I've frequently heard from many leading medical and longevity science experts I've spoken with who agree our traditional health system is "f*cked" right now.

Years pass quickly and it's hard to believe I'm now sitting here writing this third and final book. This is the end of my *Health Trilogy*, a fascinating journey I began when I kicked off my PhD research in 2009. In many respects I guess this journey really began much earlier than that when I graduated as a sport and exercise scientist in 1993. For various reasons these books became part-biographical as I used myself as the guinea pig, experimenting with various science-based techniques and technology.

My aim was to discover the truth about staying well, and identify the easiest, most effective route, to the holy grail we're all seeking – i.e. a healthier, happier, longer life <u>without the slog</u>. No diets or fitness subscriptions required. Here's the latest update on my personal wellness experiment:

As I mentioned earlier, my adoption of the simple, smart wellness habits in January 2020 extended my healthy life expectancy by 23 years in just 23 months.

That's a pretty incredible result achieved by just making small changes to my daily habits. I detailed this approach in my *Neuron* book. We've been doing the wrong thing for too long.

In the past year, since the publication of my *Neuron: Smart Wellness Made Easy* book and online programme, I've also watched others achieve the same success. This stuff works.

If you haven't yet started embedding smart wellness into your life, or are struggling to get started, I'm confident the insights I'm going to reveal in the following chapters will help you move closer to smashing your health goals.

I aim to make your journey into smart wellness even easier than ever before thanks to some of the latest longevity science insights published over recent years.

Many of these revelations are jaw droppingly shocking. I want you to read on with an open mind because some of the findings might seem hard to believe.

My intention in writing this *Health Trilogy* series is to:

- highlight and draw attention to the failed traditional approach to health

- bust open the myths we're still being sold

- challenge and disrupt this diet and fitness obsessed sector

I want to encourage you to adopt an updated mindset about the ultimate healthy lifestyle. It perhaps isn't what you imagine it is. The science has moved on. The focus is firmly on longevity and prevention because leading medical experts are now conceding that in truth, very little progress has been made over many decades. Modern medicine continues to diagnose and treat the late stage of disease. By then there is little we can do to combat the extensive damage that has accumulated invisibly beneath the surface. Real "cures" are still not on the horizon for most modern illnesses.

My first book '*The Music Diet: The Rock & Roll Guide To A Healthier, Longer Life*' was intended to draw attention to the facts and challenge and disrupt traditional thinking about health. Chapter 1 in that book listed the statistics and showed that five decades of huge diet and fitness trends failed to produce healthy nations.

As diet and fitness revenues continued to increase over the decades so did our average waistline size.

Those approaches were flawed. The book encouraged a different way of thinking about health, using natural tools that target our ancient biology. In this case, the example was music and sound.

I showcased how that aural input can deliver positive effects on our biology in a myriad of ways throughout life. Music naturally and directly hacks into our systems and therefore can help them function optimally. I was first shown how to use music to reduce anxiety, improve sleep quality and boost endurance, confidence and motivation in the early 1990s. I was a young sport and exercise science undergraduate visiting a US Naval Base in California. As a musician I was fascinated to be shown how they used music and sound as a *biohack* to reduce anxiety in high stress situations, boost physical endurance, improve sleep and more. I've been using it extensively as a tool for wellness and performance ever since. The ears lead to the brain! Our grey matter can also receive those soundwaves via our skin. Music is a supertool and my all-time favourite wellness and performance ingredient. It formed the basis of my Master's degree research examining the psycho-physical effects of music synchronisation on exercise endurance, and my PhD research examined the lifelong effects of music memories from youth. It holds phenomenal power over us due to the way our ancient brain circuitry uses sound as information.

The second book *'Neuron: Smart Wellness Made Easy'* took this discussion further. It showed how and why the habits that our brain automates can make or break our health. *Neuron* summarised all the complex science and documented the extensive 12-month experiment I ran on my own brain and body throughout 2020. I cancelled my fitness subscriptions and purely focused on adopting daily smart wellness habits for a year. As a sport and exercise scientist as well as a neuroscientist, these personal wellness results made me revisit the latest science and spurred me to radically update my thinking regarding health. **We've been getting it wrong, for too long.**

In addition to music, I also used several other habits to hack into my ancient biology to transform my weight, sleep, stress, productivity, focus and general happiness and life satisfaction.

I used a routine of simple habits such as:
- timed eating within an 8-hour window
- a diverse plant intake
- timed daylight exposure
- simple breathing techniques
- gratitude
- caffeine
- cold water
- listening to self-hypnosis recordings
- testing gut bacteria and inflammation levels
- and learning to play lead guitar like Hendrix (which actually wasn't "simple" but it was a highly effective brain building exercise!)

I pulled all this into a daily routine that efficiently targeted 6 pillars of health that I presented in the 'wheel of wellness'. I began putting others through the same programme to help them reap the same benefits.

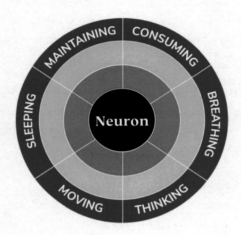

We're continually repeating the same mistakes despite their well-documented flaws. None of these things work in isolation.

- Traditional diet and fitness focused models are never going to produce a healthy nation and the scientific evidence shows the reasons for this failure

- Other wellness practices such as yoga and massage alone are also not going to produce healthy nations

- Attending a fitness or wellness session once or twice a week doesn't offset the poor habits that dominate your daily life.

- A few hours a week in a gym also don't offset the imbalanced gut microbes that are wreaking havoc 24/7.

Diet and fitness revenues increased over the decades, but so did the average waistline size and prevalence of chronic illnesses. Remember that fact.

I discussed this at length in the previous two books. There are reasons these methods aren't going to fix the problem and the real solution is now emerging in the latest science. For decades we've convinced ourselves that good health requires high effort "exercise" and restrictive, miserable, calorie counting "diets", but living a healthier, longer life is actually much simpler than we've been led to believe. In fact, it requires hardly any effort at all. At least not in the traditional way we think of 'effort'.

It's exactly 40 years since Jane Fonda's workout video became the highest selling VHS release of all-time, knocking all the Hollywood blockbuster movies into the shade. It kickstarted a series of similarly huge diet and fitness trends that continue today.

They have all failed to produce healthy nations.

The profit-based diet and fitness industries aren't going to promote this new science to you. It's not in their business interests to inform you that you don't really need to be paying their subscriptions.

Even health professionals will take years to catch up because educational curriculums are very rarely updated due to the red tape and labour-intensive nature of making substantial changes to coursework and content. I spent many years working in the academic sector. There is no incentive for a profitable educational course to make changes if paying students are continuing to flood in – if it isn't broken why change it.

Inevitably, as the scientific research continues to rapidly advance, course content becomes more and more out of date unless you're lucky enough to have a dynamic and enthusiastic tutor who personally chooses to go the extra mile and include the latest research findings in their delivery. Many tutors are so overworked with admin they don't even have the time to stay up-to-date.

We need to disrupt the old recommendations, update our thinking, and adopt a different approach health that will produce greater results. I truly believe the simple smart wellness lifestyle is the solution. It's being rapidly driven now by advances in technology. Smart tech wearables and biomarker tests such as gut tests, inflammation tests, and biological ageing rate tests, are now becoming readily available online at affordable prices.

This is what I consider to be the 'smart wellness lifestyle':

1. **Get smart**: There's a huge knowledge gap. Most of us know more about the workings of our phone than our brain and body. Learn some basic facts about your biology so you know how it works and how to look after it properly. You'll be better protected against the mistruths we're constantly surrounded by.

2. **Act smart**: Use simple biohacks and habits to help this ancient biology function properly in the confusing modern world it has to operate in

3. **Use smart wellness tech**: these wearables and bio-tests can monitor your underlying biology so you can gather info to assess how it's functioning. This valuable information helps us make adjustments, as and when necessary. This is a key part of prevention because it enables us to step in early when we see something is going wrong.

I presented this approach in my Neuron book.

- The inner green ring represents knowledge – learn how your basic biology works so you can better look after it.

- The yellow circle is the ring of habits, the simple daily things you do to help keep that biology working well.

- These are wrapped by the outer blue ring which is smart technology, wearables and bio-tech that can help you monitor how well your habits are keeping your ancient biology on track.

My goal is to help communicate these updated facts far and wide so others can benefit from them and boost their wellness in the way I have. The great news is that new cutting-edge research published in the past year has made me realise that significant wellness boosts can be achieved. We simply have to embed a range of the small habits I included in the full smart wellness model.

In this final book I'm going to help make it even easier for you to nail a lifelong wellness routine that can significantly reduce your risk of suffering from a chronic illness in the final decades of your life.

I've been watching with interest how my previous books and online content have been received and consumed.

- Some people flew through the contents of the book and online learning materials, easily adopted the smart wellness lifestyle, and transformed their approach to wellness

- Some simply didn't "get it" and didn't even begin the smart wellness journey

- Some did embark on the journey but struggled to maintain momentum by themselves. They really needed much more support to succeed in making the behavioural changes, even when they were relatively small and simple

I became fascinated by the challenge of helping everyone easily absorb this information, because I firmly believe it's life changing.

In my opinion the one, single, health supplement that we're almost all lacking is <u>KNOWLEDGE</u>. The knowledge about health we've accumulated over the past decades is largely outdated but still being promoted in public health messaging distributed by both the commercial health sector and government.

In January every year, we watch the usual fitness and diet-based adverts pepper our screens. This thinking belongs in the past. I realised though, that despite my interest in detailed analyses, I also struggle to stay focused for long periods these days. I prefer short, concise, versions of things. Bite-sized info chunks I can quickly consume.

So, that is how I'm going to present the information in this book. I'm also going to adopt this practice in my online learning materials. Short, clear, easy to understand, factual nuggets of information.

During a podcast interview in 2021, the presenter told me he loved my "verbal vitamins" and that term stuck with me. Small doses of facts can break through our attention barrier and result in changes in behaviour.

That's how this final book in my Health Trilogy will play out.

Concise.

Less is more.

Let's begin!

2

Facts

Here's the real problem

There's been a flood of very relevant new published research findings in the past few years. It turns out there are certain key drivers at a cellular level that are now becoming recognised as being associated with most of the chronic diseases that have been killing us for generations. These two below are getting particular attention.

EX-DIFFERENTIATION

&

INFLAMMATION

Ex-differentiation

During early development our cells take on distinct roles. Some become skins cells, some become brain cells etc. The DNA in those cells is spooled in a way that ensures only the code related to the normal operation of that cell type is able to be read. Think of the DNA like a hotel but the cell only has keys to access certain doors. The information inside those rooms hold the instructions for the cell to exist as whatever type it has become (e.g. skin cell).

Ex-differentiation refers to a cell becoming confused and straying from its original role. This can happen over time as damage accumulates and suddenly our epigenome in the cell is able to read parts of DNA instructions that it shouldn't really be able to access. It's not great if a skin cell can access the instructions about how to become a liver cell, for instance. A cascade of problems spiral from this situation.

Inflammation

Chronic inflammation is now recognised as being a core driver of most of the chronic illnesses we endure from middle-age onwards. The inflammatory system is a healthy function of our immune system. It's necessary to keep us well. However, it's meant to be a temporary response. When it's consistently activated, this chronic inflammation leads to other damaging problems.

Both ex-differentiation and chronic inflammation are significantly affected by our daily habits. Our lifestyles can dramatically accelerate this biological ageing process and march us towards illness. We now know our gut diversity and the health of our gut lining plays a particularly significant role as we'll discuss later.

The good news is we can actually keep these drivers in check with the habits I outlined in the smart wellness plan. The first part of the wheel of wellness – 'Consuming' - is particularly powerful. We are what we eat.

The following pages contain some basic facts (in no particular order) that are worth knowing. They're important so I've given them each their own page. They'll also be mentioned in later chapters as they interact with each other in many ways.

Leading experts now believe we only actually suffer from <u>one</u> single disease... AGEING.

This manifests in different chronic disease diagnoses depending which cells are affected by that ageing process.

9 hallmarks of ageing have been identified:

Genomic instability / telomere attrition / epigenetic alterations / loss of proteostasis / deregulated nutrient-sensing / mitochondrial dysfunction / cellular senescence / stem cell exhaustion / altered intercellular communication.

Every molecule of food and drink we pop in our mouth triggers cascades of chemical reactions that have significant effects on the cells in our brain and body.

We should not be eating any processed foods.

Our ancient biology has evolved to consume whole, natural foods only.

Everything else increases the risk of pretty disastrous long-term health consequences.

We cannot, and should not, assume that processed food and drink manufacturers, retailers, and governments, are looking after our health.

Most of the items stocked in stores are very bad for us and these retailers have their own commercial and political agendas and pressures.

Our lack of basic knowledge and understanding regarding health and nutrition puts us in danger.

e.g.
Alongside asbestos and nicotine, processed meats are on the official World Health Organisation GROUP 1 carcinogen list, because they have known links with cancer. Yet there is no law in place so far to enforce the display of warning messaging on their packaging.

Trillions of diverse bacteria should live in our gut and these colonies will decide whether you live a long, healthy life or not.

If you look after them, they look after you.

We only realised relatively recently just how crucial these little gut residents are. We've been killing most of them for generations so are now paying the price. Our gut should house a high diversity of different types of gut microbes.

Decades ago breakfast cereal manufacturers convinced us we need to eat as soon as we wake up but, for many people, extending the overnight fasting window by delaying breakfast can actually boost our biology and extend healthspan (healthy lifespan)

The damage caused by our poor habits, and stressful modern lifestyle, creeps along silently and invisibly, causing low-grade chronic inflammation until, decades later, it emerges as a chronic illness that attracts medical attention

You cannot offset the damage caused by your poor eating habits through diets or fitness.

You have to actually fix your eating habits and create a new daily routine.

Most of us don't really know how, what or when to eat because the advice is confusing, and food packaging is misleading us (sometimes deliberately)

Five decades of huge diet and fitness trends completely failed to produce healthy nations

Fitness and wellness are not the same thing and it's wellness we need, not fitness

PART ONE

F*cked

How it all failed

In talks I often refer to what I call the 3 Eras of Health.

My gran's era was the "Uninformed Era".

Doctors were featured on cigarette adverts. Tanning gadgets amplifying the strength of sun rays were promoted. The information about the damaging effects of these habits didn't arrive until much later.

My gran died a grisly smoking-related death in her 70s.

My dad's era was the "Misinformed Era".

He became obese, and suffered high cholesterol and hypertension, as processed food began to dominate modern life.

He was told that fat was the culprit and that low-fat diets and fitness were the answer. These recommendations were later proven to be incorrect. If he were alive today I'd be giving him very different advice, as we'll discuss in later pages.

He died of a fatal heart attack in a hotel celebrating his 65th birthday and retirement with my mum.

My generation is the "Informed Era".

We have access to our biological data and the science now shows us how and why it all went wrong and what we need to do. The problems actually date back millions of years before my gran's era. The following pages will trace that journey.

- 3 -

Feet

I completed my postgraduate studies in Applied Neuroscience at King's College London's Institute of Psychiatry, Psychology and Neuroscience. I found the origins of our species and our brain development particularly fascinating. Most of the medical research carried out over many decades has been conducted on other animals. Fruit flies, zebrafish, certain worms and mice share similar genetic systems to humans and can provide model insights into the workings of our own biology.

It's thought that life first originated on our planet more than 3bn years ago as microbes. That time scale is pretty hard to get your head around.

As more and more fossils are discovered around the world we are learning more about our human origins. A significant moment in our evolution was when we learnt to walk upright on our feet. Fossil records of bone structures suggest that this probably happened somewhere between 3-6 million years ago. That's fairly recent in evolutionary terms.

Walking on our feet proved to be a game-changer for a number of reasons:

- it freed up our hands to do other things like carrying things and using tools

- it drove evolutionary changes in the design of our limbs that increased efficiency

- that enabled us to walk further

46

- this in turn meant we could search further for food and increase the chance of finding some

This ability to walk upright on two feet is considered to be a crowning achievement in terms of human evolution. Recent studies provided insights into how and why we're able to do it when other primates still cannot.

We have a short area across our foot known as the transverse tarsal arch. Although this had been visibly identified a long time ago there was some confusion as to how this human anatomical feature worked. Now scientists have assigned a structure to it. This arch creates an added stiffness. This allows us to walk and run more efficiently.

- 4 -

Foragers

There are very few forager communities left in existence today, but evidence discovered by evolutionary anthropologists suggests that that hunter-gatherer culture was the normal practice for our ancient ancestors dating back 2 million years or more.

Our human biology has evolved very slowly over many millions of years so we can be sure that its evolution was driven by a foraging diet, dominated by plants because they were easier to obtain than chasing and killing animals.

You'll see in later chapters why this original nutritional habit still holds significant clues in relation to our health today. This is why evolutionary anthropologists, molecular biologists, gut microbiologists and longevity scientists from genetics and other disciplines have become so interested in tribes such as the Hadza community in Tanzania. Measuring their biology provides us with huge insights about how our Western diet has sabotaged our ancient insides. The population in western nations have noticeably lower diversity of gut bacteria than the tribes who still live the original hunter-gatherer lifestyle of our ancient ancestors.

- 5 -

Fire

Another landmark moment in our health journey came somewhere between 300,000 and 2 million years ago.

We discovered how to control fire.

Fire would have been common in the natural environment just as it spontaneously erupts today. Lightning strikes and extreme dry weather and heat can trigger fires that spread quickly. Our ancient ancestors would have witnessed this.

However, learning how to control fire delivered a lot of advantages.

It provided heat.

It provided safety at night, keeping away wild predators.

Perhaps most importantly, though, it enabled us to start cooking our food.

It is believed that this significantly boosted the level of nutrients we could consume. There are basic chemical and structural reasons for this.

When we eat raw foods the internal processes in our digestive tract have to work hard to break it down into a smaller form that can be absorbed into our blood stream when the material reaches the small intestine. This process starts with our teeth and the enzymes in our mouth, stomach and intestine that start breaking down the molecules.

On the other hand, when we heat food, that process begins before it even enters our mouth. This means we have to spend less energy breaking it down and it gives us a greater opportunity to extract more of the nutrients from that food.

This gave us an energy boost and enabled us to build more cells.

- 6 -

Frontal lobe

Our brains have evolved steadily over the past 6 million years. At first the growth was pretty insubstantial but, from 800,000 to 200,000 years ago, our ancestors' brain size increased rapidly. There is no conclusive evidence for why or how this happened, but we know that our brain is an extremely energy-hungry structure. It requires a lot of fuel. This fuel has to be consumed via the food we eat and digest.

It makes sense that our gradual use of fire for cooking could have also contributed to this growth. It enabled us to extract and convert more nutrients into fuel.

The frontal lobe is the most recent part of our brain to evolve. Not all regions of the frontal lobe experienced equal growth though. The pre-frontal cortex at the front of the lobe grew much larger than the motor cortex region at the rear. The pre-frontal cortex is the region housing neurons which play a significant role in planning, decision-making, personality, and social communication.

This growth spurt also coincided with a period of dramatic climate change. It would have been an advantage to have a frontal lobe featuring a larger, more highly-evolved, pre-frontal cortex to help figure out how to live in those extreme conditions and survive.

In terms of comparative neuroanatomy, this enlargement of the pre-frontal cortex makes our amazing human brain much more sophisticated than just a larger version of a monkey brain.

Fungi?

Another hypothesis regarding the development of our brain is the 'Stoned Ape Theory' presented by Terrence and Dennis McKenna in 1992. They proposed that the addition of mushrooms to our ancestors diet might have helped with the reorganisation of parts of our brain, leading us to higher consciousness and imagination. This may have been due to the psilocybin properties of the mushrooms.

Interestingly, psilocybin is now being heralded for its neurological benefits. After having previously been outlawed due to its drug classification and recreational use in past decades, it's now back in the mainstream. There are an increasing number of trials and companies showing how it can be more effective than prescribed pharmaceuticals for many individuals suffering from mental illnesses, such as treatment-resistant depression.

Farmers

Our brilliant frontal lobe and the super-brilliant pre-frontal cortex within it, gave us the ability to start having many sophisticated ideas. We were able to solve problems, find solutions, use logic and plan ahead.

One of our ideas about 12,000 years ago was to become farmers instead of foragers.

This does indeed seem a brilliant idea.

Growing our own plants and rearing animals meant that we no longer had to walk so far to hunt and gather our food sources. We could simply stay in one place.

This helped ensure a steadier supply of food and reduced the likelihood of us having to be hungry for days when our foraging efforts failed to find food.

However, in hindsight, our shift from foraging to farming is potentially when it all started to go a bit "tits up", as I'll explain in the coming pages.

- 8 -

Flora & Fauna

Tracking, hunting and killing animals required effort, sometimes requiring days of activity. Often with no prize at the end. Meat wasn't an everyday food item on the menus of our ancient ancestors, however, breeding and rearing animals in captive environments provided a much higher likelihood of regular meat for consumption. Our meat-eating habit was able to increase when farming became the common lifestyle.

We did also grow plants but the types of plants we grew were limited in number compared with the diversity growing in the natural environment. According to the Food and Agriculture Organisation of the United States there are more than 50,000 edible plant species known in the world. There are doubtless many more that we have not yet identified. However, the staggering statistic is that we grow so few of them as crops. Approximately 90 percent of the world's food intake is provided by just 15 crop plants. Maize, rice and wheat dominate the global populations intake and are the three staple foods for more than 4 billion people.

Gradually, our meat eating has increased and our plant eating (and diversity) has decreased.

I mentioned on previous pages that even the last remaining hunter-gatherer tribes today have a much higher diversity of gut microbes than the rest of us. This is unsurprising when you see what a narrow range of crops we decided to grow. This narrow reliance on so few species makes us vulnerable. Climate change, new pests and new diseases could present significant challenges in coming years. Consequently, there has been a call for more diversity and the greater use of less commonly grown edible plants.

A few years ago, a body more than 5,000 years old was found in ice in Europe. Due to the mummification effect of the ice it was possible to analyse the gut bacteria present at the time of death. It's believed this man lived a part farmer / part forager lifestyle. This isn't surprising as this transition would have happened over a long period and over several generations. His gut microbes were more diverse than ours today.

Furniture

A few thousand years ago we invented chairs. It seemed like a good idea, but we now blame many of our modern health issues on the extensive amount of time we spend sitting down every day - the so-called "sedentary lifestyle". Chairs aren't a modern invention but our shift towards office working in recent centuries has meant we now spend more time sitting in these pieces of furniture than our ancestors did.

From an evolutionary perspective, it's interesting to acknowledge that today's hunter-gatherer communities also spend quite a lot of time at rest but there are important differences.

Studies of the Hadza tribe show that they spend some time sitting on the ground but also a lot of time in the kneeling and squatting position. The bones of our pelvis don't lend themselves to long periods of sitting on hard surfaces. After a while it becomes increasingly uncomfortable. This is why our ancestors made cushioned seats so we could sit on our bony butts for longer. Our increasingly sophisticated designs have made the chair one of the most common pieces of furniture and we spend large portions of our day sitting in them.

This isn't how our evolutionary anatomy was designed though. The resting squat is a much more natural position for us but we hardly ever adopt that position in modern life. Importantly, it's also the natural position when defecating but we turned our toilets into chairs and began adopting a sitting position on the loo.

All this sitting isn't good for us for various reasons.

Firstly, whenever our bodyweight is taken by an object, our musculature is able to dial down. Compare this to a resting squat position where your muscles are constantly having to fire with a low hum of activity to maintain that position. There's a much higher energy effect.

Secondly, sitting alters the anal-rectal angle which isn't helpful when trying to poop. The resting squat is a much more natural position for pooping. It actually remains the standard poop position in much of the eastern world today. Whereas, the West decided that sitting on a toilet as if it were a chair was seemingly more dignified and represented a class distinction. There are now some schools of thought suggesting a potential link between our western pooping position and various chronic issues of the rectal canal but this is not proven.

- 10 -

Fertilisers

As we began to increase our farming activity this brought new challenges. Continuously growing crops on the same land inevitably impacts the fertility of that soil. Our early ancestors realised this as their yield would have been in decline. This would have led to starvation or a return to the hunter-gatherer foraging lifestyle of moving around a larger area rather than living in one place.

Plants need five essentials for growth: sunlight, water, potassium, phosphorous and nitrogen. In the natural environment this process is seamless because when the plants die they return their nitrogen to the soil which new plants then use for growth. However, when we became farmers we disrupted this natural cycle. The plants don't die and decompose. We harvest them and take them away for our own use. Nitrogen levels in that soil decline.

Rotating the use of land helped the soil rest and recuperate. Eventually though, our smart ancestors started using manure to help keep the soil fertile so that land continued to yield a healthy supply of crops. There are several theories relating to this. It's thought that keeping herds and growing crops would have happened on the same land so, it would have been noticeable that crops grew well in areas where dung accumulated.

There are differing views regarding when exactly this practice would have begun but there is some evidence dating back 8,000 years. Plants treated with manure have higher levels of a nitrogen isotope. Plant remains from archeological farming sites found in Europe seem to suggest manure was being used in this organised way. Regular spreading of manure would have enabled long-term use of land for crop farming because it breaks down slowly over many years. Farmers also realised that nitrogen could be returned to the soil in other ways. Compost works nicely. The roots of legumes also contain bacteria which help boost nitrogen levels, so including peas or beans in crop rotation is helpful. Lightning also helps deliver nitrates to the soil via rain fall but this couldn't be called upon reliably.

All these natural techniques certainly helped our farming lifestyle but the real fertiliser breakthrough came much later. In the early 20th century a German scientist worked out how to transform nitrogen in the air into a form that could be used on soil. Extreme heat and pressure break the bonds between nitrogen atoms in the air which are then able to bond with hydrogen, producing ammonia. Synthetic fertiliser is now produced in staggering quantities to drive our demand for large and continuous crop yields.

Environmentalists and health organisations today are calling for more investigations into the damaging effects of overuse of these chemical fertilisers on soil, and the associated impact on water quality, health and the natural environment. However, our enormous demand for food for humans, combined with the vast amount of crops needed for animal feed, makes it difficult to move away from using fertilisers. Our mass production expectations are high and deeply embedded in our food system.

- 11 -

Factory Foods

Farming and production of commercial fertilisers gave us the ability to mass produce food. Prior to that we were mainly producing for ourselves or our local community in quantities sufficient for survival. Practices to process and preserve food date back millions of years. Heating food over fire is a form of processing. Smoking, salting and fermenting are forms of preservation. Eventually, though, we learnt how to take these practices to a much larger scale, mainly for monetary gain.

The food industry has grown extensively since the 19th Century. A method called pasteurisation was developed in the 1800s by French biologist, Louis Pasteur. This technique used heat to kill microbes but didn't spoil the taste or nutritional quality of the food. This was a significant breakthrough because it enabled the long-term storage and transportation of food.

The invention of airtight tin can and jars also proved to be a turning point in food history because it provided a sealed environment and offered long-term food supplies. Tinned food was a staple diet for the military in the 20th Century world wars.

Factories soon popped up to churn out these products. Ready meals also began to emerge as manufacturers recognised the appeal of convenience foods in an increasingly demanding lifestyle.

All this mass production further fuelled the use of fertilisers so farmers could keep pace with the demand from the factories.

In just a few hundred years food production has turned into an industry that generated more than $8 trillion in global revenue in 2021, an increase of over half a trillion dollars in 12 months.

Sadly, most of these foods and drinks that now surround us on a daily basis in every shop, workplace, school and hospital are actually not good for our health. They are quietly causing grave damage to our ancient cellular processes that we'll revisit again in later pages in this book. Our consuming habits are accelerating our biological ageing rate and marching us towards decades of chronic illness in later life.

- 12 -

Food Fraud

I'm going to keep this short as I simply want to make you aware of it. This is a real thing. The Royal Society for Public Health ran a webinar for members on this topic last year.

It's a growing concern and we are all falling victim to it when we shop.

The rise of processed foods in factories delivered a new and superb marketing opportunity – printed labels.

These physical products become branded with colours, images and words. These are often misleading and misrepresentative. Foods that appear to be healthy are often not.

They feature smiling faces and words we associate with energy and wellness. It's become common practice and is largely unregulated. Governments have insisted on ingredients and nutrient profiles being listed but for most people these are meaningless. Their purchasing decision is driven by the label and the TV adverts.

The advertising industry boomed after World War II. More homes were buying television sets and had disposable income. The food and drink industry and advertising industry worked hand in hand and reaped the rewards.

They still do today.

So, beware.

- 13-

Fat

Our parents and grandparents were bombarded by this constant, convenient, availability of delicious processed foods and drinks. Factories were mass producing and investing in sophisticated production lines and new technology. Supermarkets were popping up in our towns and cities, stocking vast ranges of product ranges for us to feast on. We had foods from around the world and could simply pop it in the microwave or oven and eat it in front of the TV which featured endless processed food adverts.

Eating and drinking became a huge deal.

Our consumption habits increased.

Portion sizes increased.

So did our waistlines.

We became fat thanks to our body's superb ability to convert and hold almost endless quantities in our adipose storage tissues, an ancient process intended to help us survive famine periods.

As our weight increased so did our health problems.

We continued to eat and drink and as the recipes were formulated to trigger our brain's reward system, these consumption patterns became hard to stop.

Several studies examined the issue to find the answers. Fat was blamed as the culprit. It provides more than twice the amount of calories per gram than carbohydrates or proteins.

"This must be the reason!" some health experts declared.

"Avoid fat!"

A wave of "low-fat" and "fat-free" products began to be produced to target the overweight population who were keen to try and reverse the damage. A growing tsunami of these product ranges appeared on shelves and refrigerators in our stores.

Low-fat diets were recommended by health professionals.

We now know this advice was flawed.

It actually made the problem even worse as you'll see in the following pages.

We need healthy fat in our diet. It's the unhealthy fat that was and is the problem. Advising people to veer away from fat resulted in an even greater intake of carbohydrate foods and sugar. This became even more dangerous as we'll discuss in the next chapter.

- 14 -

Fructose Corn Syrup (high)

The processed food industry became a big commercial business in a relatively short period of time.

Commercial business is about profit.

Profits can be increased in various ways. You can increase the sales volume of the product, or increase the price of the product, or cut the manufacturing cost of the product.

The food corporation giants had realised that our ancient brain particularly loves sugar. This ingredient is difficult for us to ignore because it triggers ancient neural pathways that evolved over millions of years and were intended to help ensure our survival.

Even today our brain loves sugar so much that the world's last remaining hunter-gatherer communities continue risking their safety to climb trees and gather honey from beehives.

However, in the processed food sector, sugar (sucrose) as a natural ingredient is expensive. So, when manufacturers learnt about a new ingredient developed in the late 1950s they were keen to experiment with it. This product was high fructose corn syrup (HFCS). It was soon being pumped into processed food products, especially sugary drinks and desserts.

The "low-fat" health recommendations actually resulted in pushing us towards an increased intake of carbohydrates and HCFS. This eating habit is now known to have detrimental effects on our health and our weight.

In truth we do actually need fats and sugars in moderate amounts. Certain fats are an essential part of our healthy diet and our primary energy fuel is sugar (glucose). However, our new factory foods were dominated by unhealthy saturated fats, unhealthy sugar levels and HFCS.

A few years ago documents published by the JAMA Internal Medicine journal revealed that the sugar industry paid scientists at Harvard in the 1960s to publish a review that promoted saturated fat as the culprit of the rising obesity-related health crisis. The sugar industry selected the studies that were used in the review.

For many decades health professionals continued to follow this advice, encouraging people to stay away from fat. This pushed them towards increasing consumption of the low-fat, high sugar foods and drinks, that many experts now blame for the obesity crisis we continue to witness today.

- 15 -

Fitness

As the diet industry recommendations continued to fail and waistlines and health problems continued to rise we turned to a new solution. FITNESS!

The exercise industry absolutely boomed as it began to target the population with its promise to "burn" off the fat.

As a sport and exercise scientist in the 1990s, I myself also believed this claim was true. I built a very successful health club chain for a family hotel business. It was eventually sold for £180M.

The fitness format is a great business model. Thanks to the endless health promotions urging people to take up fitness, a steady stream of people walk into your gym in January when they set their new year resolutions. They set up their monthly direct debit. Their motivation fizzles out by March because they don't really see results and haven't really got time to squeeze gym visits into their already hectic lives. Their guilt stops them from cancelling the direct debit though.

The fitness and exercise-to-music industry skyrocketed through the 1980s and 1990s and continues to be profitable today. It has consistently grown.

Fitness revenues continued to grow.

Average waistline size and the obesity-related health crisis continued to grow too.

These claims of using fitness to burn off the excess calories and fat stores simply weren't fulfilling the promise.

Why?

There's been some very interesting evolutionary anthropology research published in recent years. Herman Pontzer from Duke University has been a lead figure in this field. Advances in field research methods and technology have enabled total energy expenditure to be measured on a daily basis, while participants go about their daily business. This is done by giving them a special type of water in the morning and then collecting their urine. The information gathered can tell us how many kilocalories were burned as energy during the day. This includes not just energy used from movement, but also energy used through all the other metabolism and cellular jobs the brain and body carries out every day. Even digesting the food we eat, and thinking, require energy.

When I graduated in the 1990s we believed that the more you exercised the more calories you burned. Therefore, fat stores would be used up. This is the science that continues to be promoted by many fitness professionals today.

However, the new research gives a very different insight into our metabolism. Our ancient biology is very clever. It compensates. Pontzer's studies have shown that hunter-gatherers who are extremely active on a daily basis (often clocking up 19,000 steps during a day) actually don't really burn much more energy than a typical adult in the western world who is fairly sedentary. It appears our metabolism has a ceiling. There is a general limit in the amount of calories we are able to metabolise, so our body has to decide where to direct that energy. This has significant implications for exercise and health because it means that if we are frequently forcing our body to do extra physical activity it has to compensate by redirecting energy that would have otherwise been used elsewhere.

If this energy diversion means your immune system, or cellular repair activity, gets dialled down so the calories can be used for your treadmill session, you're potentially having a negative impact on your health.

It's clear that fitness and wellness are not the same thing. This is something I frequently stated in my previous book – *Neuron: Smart Wellness Made Easy.*

It's also clear that fitness doesn't burn off the fat problem and fix the health crisis.

If it did we wouldn't be in the situation we are today.

Yet the common health advice for weight loss still given today is "join a gym and do fitness". It's a myth.

We need to update these recommendations.

- 16 -

Fads & Fashion

Five decades of fitness failed to produce healthy nations but along the way some of the biggest brands and celebrities in popular cultural history have been built.

Jane Fonda was already a movie star, but when her workout video topped the charts and became an all-time best seller, she reached new audiences and new heights. Many other TV fitness personalities have been built on their fitness credentials.

We've also cycled through many new trends over the decades.

Aerobics.

Aqua aerobics.

Step.

Body Pump.

Zumba.

(...just to name a few)

Various machines and equipment have also entered the arena over the years with promises of "results". Everything from the original "Bullworker" chest expander to today's Peloton bike and a myriad of items in between.

It wasn't just the fitness clubs and brands that enjoyed lucrative revenue streams. They also spawned a huge fashion industry dedicated to producing clothes specifically for workouts.

That exercise gear gradually seeped into the mainstream as just ordinary clothing styles that people could wear in everyday settings, not just in a gym. Who could forget the infamous "legwarmer" era, or the sweatbands sported by Olivia Newton-John in her "Physical" music video.

Fitness and sports fashion continues to boom today. The stores occupy hugely expensive, prime location, real-estate in almost every major city in the world.

Wearing fitness gear does not solve the health crisis, though.

"Farma"
(forgive the F cheat)

As the diet and fitness industries continued to fail to fix the health crisis and the food and drink industry continued to fuel it, we turned to another potential solution – "pharma"

Increasing levels of pharmaceuticals began being prescribed by doctors to help treat the symptoms of the chronic illnesses suffered by their patients.

The pharma industry is absolutely colossal and continues to grow. Many drugs produce side effects that eventually require another drug. Additionally, these drugs don't really address the underlying issue that's driving the illness. By the time the patient has noticed symptoms and got around to making an appointment they're likely to already be at a late stage of the chronic disease. These conditions often begin at a low cellular level for years and decades before any noticeable symptoms arise. The prescribed drugs combat the problem.

Drugs for high blood pressure artificially manage the situation.

Drugs for Type-II diabetes artificially manage the situation.

They don't solve the situation.

They aren't designed to target the underlying cause of the problem.

The patients often continue to eat and drink as they had before. Beneath the surface more damage is being done.

The pharmaceutical industry is a commercial sector. There are huge profits at stake. It's all about sales. Drug companies SELL to the medical professionals that prescribe them. In previous decades they also offered attractive incentives and swanky lunches to try and further encourage the prescription of their products.

For decades there has been a constant stream of customers available for these pharmaceutical products as we continue to gain weight and suffer the related chronic health effects.

Medical professionals and health organisations are now trying to move away from this "pharma first" model.

Prevention is better than prescription.

- 18 -

FAIL

F*ck!

Fat-free diets failed.

Fitness failed.

Farma failed.

WTF?!

We're at a turning point. A new era is dawning. It was already rising but the global COVID-19 pandemic fuelled it. It's obvious we can't keep trying the same things when history has shown that they are flawed, wrong and don't work.

We need to learn from the past and shift quickly to a different approach built on the new science.

Twenty years ago my dad died of a fatal heart attack, in a hotel, celebrating his 65th birthday and retirement with my mum. It followed years of obesity and high blood pressure. He'd failed to follow any of the diet or fitness recommendations that both his doctor and I had been urging him to adopt. It now turns out those recommendations were actually flawed. If I were having that conversation with him today I would give him completely different advice. He would now be almost 90 years old, a completely achievable healthy age.

This is an important point because if he were speaking with a doctor or fitness instructor today they would not be giving him the recommendations that I would be giving him. They'd likely be still giving him the outdated advice. This is because the new science is not yet common practice across the medical world or fitness industry. It hasn't yet seeped out of the scientific journals. There are some doctors and fitness professionals who are personally seeking and seizing this new knowledge and are beginning to adopt it in their practices. In general, though, these people are few and far between at present.

We need to ensure this new knowledge gets out to everyone as quickly as possible. That's what I hope this final book in my Health Trilogy will help achieve. There are a growing number of experts also promoting this updated information. Part One of this book showed you our journey over the past 6 million years and how we ended up in the health crisis we experience today. Part Two of this book will give you an overview of the new science, the new recommendations, and show you how to increase your change of enjoying a long and health future, avoiding the chronic diseases that sadly shortened the healthy lives of our parents and grandparents.

PART TWO

Future

How to make it F'ing Fabulous (and long)

Our evolution and development has been driven by our ability to learn from past experiences and use new knowledge to make updated decisions.

Science moves on.

We no longer watch black and white televisions. We embraced the colour technology because it's better.

We no longer travel by foot or horse and cart. We switched to planes, trains and automobiles because they're better.

We no longer cook over fires because ovens are better.

We no longer use dial up internet modems because broadband and fibre optic internet connections are better.

We no longer use our landline telephones because mobile phones are better.

We no longer put up with scratched CDs because streaming music is easier and gives access to extensive music collections.

You get the picture.

We embrace the applied science and technological advancements as they evolve.

So, why are we still using outdated diet and fitness recommendations? Science-based studies and health data clearly show they don't work.

Also, why are we still eating a daily diet dominated by processed and ultra-processed foods when the evidence shows the damage they cause?

Over the past 12 months I've been running a small in-house longevity study as part of the R&D of my Neuron Wellness start-up company. Behavioural change is our core objective, so I've been observing the biological ages and habits of a range of people, and seeing what (if anything motivates them to take action and make small adjustments to their daily routines). This work was carried out in partnership with our colleagues at GlycanAge who are doing phenomenal work in the biological age testing field. It presented useful insights that have helped inform the development of my smart wellness programme.

Here's a glimpse into some of the findings:

Many people's biological age was significantly older than their chronological age, especially women aged over 50 who were not on hormone replacement therapy. This isn't unusual as oestrogen positively influences anti-inflammatory responses. Consequently, as this hormone declines through perimenopause and menopause, women's biological ageing rate can accelerate much faster than men's. Hence why I am particularly keen to help communicate this vital information to women in my age group. They are at higher risk. Some women don't experience this acceleration due to their genetics, but many do, and because it's invisible chronic inflammation at a cellular level they are not actually aware it is happening until a chronic disease is diagnosed further down the line.

Individuals we tested who had a regular high level fitness routine, and/or had experienced chronic and acute stress, also demonstrated accelerated ageing. Both of those factors have the ability to drive chronic inflammation.

Examples:
- Male aged 55, with a biological age of 76.
- Female, aged 56, with a biological age of 64.

Individuals who were either already following the principles of the smart wellness programme, or adopted the smart wellness habits, showed a lower biological age.

Examples:
- Male, aged 82, biological age of 46.
- Male, aged 61, biological age of 25.
- Female, aged 50, biological age of 32.

One participant also regained control of her chronic fatigue syndrome / ME condition and was able to return to work.

It's evident that our lifestyle can destroy our biology and accelerate ageing, but small habit adjustments can reverse the damage and significantly reduce our risk of future chronic disease.

The study also showed that some people find it relatively easy to make small changes to their routine. Others struggled to maintain the motivation to successfully adjust their habits. Some individuals were unable to take any small steps towards change at all. Often not even able to commit to watching the short instructional videos we gave them access to.

These insights made me realise that even though in my Neuron book I brought tonnes of science-based information into a single programme, it was still too much information for some people. So, I went back to the drawing board and tried to simplify everything even further. My hope is that everyone will be able to start at the most basic point and as they become more interested, they will become interested to discover more information and make further changes.

The following pages will help you embrace the new science and get up to speed with the most basic habit adjustments for longevity.

- 19 -

Factors of Longevity

I was first introduced to the 'Yamanaka Factors' during my Applied Neuroscience studies at King's College London that I completed after my PhD. Shinya Yamanaka MD, PhD, was awarded the Nobel Prize in Physiology and Medicine in 2012 for discovering them.

In basic terms, cells differentiate in early development and become distinct cells. In other words, some become skin cells, some become liver cells etc. In 2006, Yamanaka and colleagues showed that a combination of certain genes (factors) could reprogramme a differentiated cell to give it the ability to self-renew as other types of cells. These are called induced pluripotent stem cells. This was a significant turning point in the medical world and is a fast-moving core field in longevity and ageing science right now.

This discovery doesn't just hold potential for modern disease treatment. It also opens a whole new world of opportunity to combat ageing.

Since 2020, there has been increasing activity in this field. Researchers are demonstrating that partial reprogramming of cells using some of the Yamanaka Factors does rejuvenate ageing cells. Now billions of dollars of research funding are being poured into this anti-ageing (geroscience) field to explore whether ethical and safe ways of bringing this into mainstream are possible. Alternative methods that don't require use of Yamanaka Factors are also being explored (because using the Yamanaka Factors exposes a risk of accidentally completely erasing the cell identity).

It's not out of the scope of reality to envisage a "reset" service in future where this therapy could reverse the age of your cells, giving you decades of additional healthy lifespan. If they discover this reset technique can be repeated multiple times who knows how long we might be able to live healthily. Perhaps, far beyond 100 years old. We are already living this long but in not great health and kept alive with a daily cocktail of pharmaceuticals in care homes. How does lengthening our healthy life expectancy impact pension funds? Can you afford to live longer?

These cellular reset breakthroughs may become an achievable reality in our lifetime, but for now it makes sense to take some other precautions just in case they do not.

This brings me back to the pathways of longevity I mentioned back at the start of this book. There are simple lifestyle changes that we can implement today to target some, or all, of the 9 identified hallmarks of ageing we mentioned previously. They are shown in the following diagram. Many of them are inter-related so improving one can help improve others too.

*From "The Hallmarks of Aging" by Lopez-Otin et al
(2013), Cell, Volume 153, Issue 6, p 1194-1217.*

I'm not going to discuss these hallmarks in detail in this book (perhaps the Health Trilogy will need to become a "Quadrilogy"!) but here are some key points I want to bring to your attention right now.

Firstly, our lifestyles have consequences. In other words, our habits and environments influence how our genes are expressed and how optimally these epigenetic processes are performing their functions. This becomes critical when relating to the maintenance of the cell because accumulating damage eventually causes cell death, or results in senescent cells that are no longer functioning but are also not killed and cleared. They become zombie cells, sending out damaging signalling molecules and causing greater disruption.

Secondly, if cellular ageing is our main health problem and is greatly influenced by our habits and environment, we can quite easily address it with some relatively simple changes to our daily routine.

Thirdly, nutrition is a particularly important driver of these hallmarks of ageing because of the role of nutrient sensing pathways.

Longevity Pathways

Leading longevity scientists have in recent years been focusing in on certain cellular pathways as proposed key mechanisms that can accelerate or slow the ageing process. They play particularly vital roles in terms of cell repair (autophagy) and energy regulation (cell metabolism).

The three types of proteins associated with these pathways are:

- AMPK
- mTOR
- Sirtuins

I believe we're going to be hearing more and more about these "three amigos" in the coming years – they are our friends and we need to nurture and appreciate them. We also need to respect the value of NAD which is the main fuel source of sirtuins. These systems are closely interlinked and regulated by nutrient levels and as you saw in the 9 hallmarks of ageing, deregulated nutrient sensing is one of the reasons for cellular disruption.

I titled this book "Longevity Made Easy" so I'm not going to delve into the molecular biology. I don't think it's necessary here. I just want to help you understand how to change our habits to influence these pathways if they're so vital. However, I will at a later point be producing various videos online that discuss the processes in detail if you're interested.

For now, this is what I think we all should be aware of:

As mentioned above, those pathways are nutrient sensors so embedding regular fasting periods into your routine is a particularly effective way of influencing their activity. The beneficial effects of AMPK, mTOR and sirtuins are boosted when we are in adverse conditions. The following pages will explain this in more detail.

Leading medical experts worldwide are now aligning around the fact that prevention is better than cure. It's far preferable to stop the first cancer cell from ever forming than try to eliminate it once it's in full swing.

It's much smarter to directly target these longevity pathways in the cells with our daily habits (and supplements if required) to keep them working well, slowing the inevitable ageing process as cells continue to divide throughout life.

- 20 -

Famine, Flight, Freeze, Frazzle

As I mentioned previously, these longevity pathways are activated by adverse conditions. Actions that recreate these adverse conditions have recently become termed as "adversity mimetics" which I think is a good term to describe them. It basically means that we are imitating adversity to trigger the cellular response. This involves doing things that mimic conditions that our ancient evolutionary biology recognises as signals we're entering a tough situation and focuses in on building resilience at a cellular level in order to survive.

Four ways of doing this are:

1. Famine

As AMPK, mTOR and the sirtuins are influenced by nutrient levels in the cells and the blood it makes sense to use our food intake as a tool when targeting them. Simply delaying your breakfast to allow an extended overnight fasting window can not only directly influence available nutrient levels but it can also help maintain healthy insulin sensitivity. Avoiding sugary and refined carbohydrate foods also help us avoid blood glucose spikes and protect our liver and cells from excessive glucose and insulin exposure.

Extending your overnight fasting period to 16+ hours is a very simple habit to adopt because you're asleep for most of this period. Simply enjoy a healthy meal the day before and then don't eat again the following day until 16 hours later. This method is also often referred to as 16:8 intermittent fasting, or time restricted eating, and it's something I discussed in more detail in my Neuron book and smart wellness programme. Studies have shown that embedding this 8-hour window earlier in the day also works. However, from a modern lifestyle perspective, most of my clients and I find it much easier to delay breakfast than avoid eating dinner.

Our modern life gives most of us a lifestyle of abundance where plenty of food is within easy reach. Consequently, we eat too often and too much. This means those vital adversity pathways aren't triggered in the way they were designed. It's essential that we contrast periods of abundance with periods of adversity to trigger these pathways so they can do the essential maintenance work in our cells. Adopting a simple fasting practice is a highly effective way of doing this. We just have to eat healthily, with a diverse range of plants and all the other essentials (fish / omega 3s / protein sources etc), within your 8-hour eating window. I now do this as normal practice. It's fine to have days off too. I do this Monday to Friday and ease up the routine at weekends otherwise life would start to suck a little. If I have events during the week I also don't fret about it. I just get back into the routine the next day.

2. Flight

Just as fasting mimics a potential upcoming famine, high intensity bursts of activity mimic flight from danger. This physical movement also alters cell nutrient levels due to the level of fuel required. So, get out of breath a few times a week doing something you love. Or just get into the habit of taking the stairs instead of the lift. Or add a steep hill into your dog walking route. Any movement that produces a high level of exertion over a short time period can activate these adversity pathways and trigger them into action. The rapid depletion of stored glycogen triggers signalling molecules that our nervous system recognises as an alert. There are some really interesting high efficiency gadgets available now that help mimic this response. The bicycle we now use in our Neuron smart wellness hub uses artificial intelligence to produce this effect in just two 20-second bursts of high intensity cycling. It's so fast and efficient that you don't have time to get hot or sweat. Therefore, no workout gear or showers are required. It's just in our bar area. Most people who have a gym habit are not actually doing exercise that produces this effect. During all my "mystery shopper" visits to many leading fitness chains I have on every occasion been given outdated advice that isn't really worth following in terms of producing longevity outcomes. You'd get greater benefits from simply going for a walk outdoors every day and focusing in on other aspects of wellness such as your consuming habits and sleep quality.

3. Freeze

Another method of recreating adversity is cold exposure. There are several ways of doing this depending on how keen you and how much money you are prepared to spend. Personally, I just have cold showers (turning the temperature to cold before exiting) and swim in the sea because I live at the beach so have easy access to it. You could also use ice baths or cryo-chambers but not everyone can afford or access those. Exposure to cold is a simple way to expose your cellular biology to an extreme temperature stressor and kick those longevity pathways into gear.

4. Frazzle

Similarly, another way to expose yourself to an extreme temperature stressor is by using high heat. Saunas have long been used to boost health. There are now also some great infra-red sauna options that make it a lot easier and cheaper to do this. To get even greater benefits rotate between the heat and cold exposure. For example, traditional saunas have had icy plunge pools nearby to allow this hot-cold-hot-cold method. My town is hopefully getting a great sauna cabin installed on the actual beach meaning we can get hot and sweaty and then throw ourselves in the sea. That will be amazing. It's arrival has been delayed due to planning regulations – another example of how outdated we are in our thinking. The significant health benefits of this installation are being overlooked.

- 21-

Fermented Foods

My first experience of fermented foods was German sauerkraut, and I must confess I wasn't a fan. I had to hide my initial response to not offend my German colleagues who enthusiastically ordered it for me in the restaurant. It's become a staple food in Germany but it apparently originated many thousands of years ago in China. This sour cabbage dish was the fuel of workers building the Great Wall of China (along with rice). This fermenting practice was commonplace and gave foods extra stability and longevity. Today fermented foods and drinks are back in favour due to their beneficial effects on our gut diversity. I predict that shelves in stores are going to become filled with extensive selections of fermented food and drink products in the coming years.

Recent research has discovered the potential link between gut diversity and risk of chronic disease. The new recommendations emerging from this research now advise a weekly intake of at least 30 different types of plants in order to boost and maintain a more diverse gut microbiome featuring many different species. We'll discuss this in more detail when we look at fibre and examine the importance of prebiotic foods (materials that the gut microbes feed on and convert into metabolites that are essential for our own healthy functioning).

Fermented foods, on the other hand, are probiotic. This means they are full of live bacteria.

There are two ways to achieve and maintain a highly diverse gut microbiome.

1. Eat and drink fermented foods so you're putting new live bacteria into your gut

2. Eat a diverse range of prebiotic fibre (plants) so that the bacteria thrive and multiply

I reintroduced fermented sauerkraut into my regular nutritional consumption during my 12-month experiment, documented in the Neuron book. It was far more delicious than I remembered. In fact, I now love it. Note: if the sauerkraut you buy is on a supermarket shelf and not in a chiller it probably doesn't contain sufficient live bacteria to be considered a probiotic.

There are several other ways of consuming live bacteria through fermented foods. Kimchi is another great option if you like something with a bit more of a fiery kick. Some blue cheese also contains live bacteria and so does miso.

Some drinks and dairy products also have probiotic live bacterial contents, such as kefir and kombucha. In July 2022, I opened a Live Bacteria Bar at our new Neuron office. In the 9 months of research leading up to that opening, I watched as more and more kombucha and kefir brands started emerging and rapidly growing in the marketplace. There is clearly a new wave emerging – just as the small independent brewers drove the craft ale wave in previous years. I could easily have stocked around 100 different brands and flavours of kombucha drinks. I've also been exploring the possibility of making my own. It'll be interesting to see how this boom progresses. It would not surprise me if Coca-Cola or one of the other major drinks corporations bought one or more of these independent kombucha and kefir manufacturers within the next year.

Kombucha is a healthy drink, although it does contain sugar. King's College London are currently examining the contents of a range of consumer kombuchas, and it will be interesting to read their findings regarding the level of health benefits. Many people I speak with tell me they didn't like kombucha when they tried it. I urge you to try it again. Independent fermenters have really worked hard to improve the flavour profiles without destroying the probiotic health effects. There are lots of delicious ones now available.

Several employer clients have mentioned their concern about energy drinks consumption to me in meetings this year. These high caffeine, high sugar drinks have become the norm in the workplace (and in schools) and are heavily overused. If we can position kombucha as a replacement habit that would bring benefits not just to gut health but also in reducing the excess caffeine reliance. Just as alcohol can have a place in a healthy lifestyle, these energy drink aren't harmful if used respectfully. They can actually produce positive effects when consumed in the right way at the right time (especially in terms of performance). Unfortunately though many consumers drink them morning, noon and night and that habit has eventual consequences and impairs both wellness and performance.

Find a few brands of fermented foods that you really enjoy and include them in your routine every day.

Fibre

As mentioned on previous pages, once you've put the live bacteria into your gut, via various fermented foods and drinks, it's vital to feed them. We focus a lot on foods that as humans we need to absorb. This takes place in the small intestine where our nutritional molecules are extracted from the things we eat and drink. They pass through into our blood stream and are transported to the liver and cells around the body.

However, we're not the only organism that needs fuel. Our gut microbes also need fuel in order to survive long enough to produce the metabolites we need for our human biology, and to reproduce so their offspring can continue the job. Some of these microbes have a very short lifespan of less than an hour. These guys are literally running a chemical factory down in our lower intestine by converting the prebiotic fibre we consume into the molecules we need for gut lining maintenance, immune function and more. The short chain fatty acids they produce are a core element of our healthy functioning. As we've mentioned before, diversity of plants is key. Unlike other nutrients, prebiotic fibre does not get absorbed into our blood stream as it passes through. It continues the journey to the large intestine where the majority of our gut bugs are waiting in eager anticipation.

Fibre also helps act as a barrier in our small intestine, slowing down the absorption of other nutrients that have to battle past it to get through the gut wall into our circulation. This is very helpful because when we eat a meal containing lots of refined carbohydrates, or sugar drinks, it would otherwise pass through the wall very quickly, sending a tidal wave of glucose to the liver and causing a spike of insulin to be released. Eating fibre as part of your meal helps provide this buffer to slow that absorption rate, as well as progressing on to eventually feed the gut bacteria. This is a reason I'm not a great fan of juicing. Drinking the juice without the pulp sends floods of sugar without fibre into your small intestine and towards your liver. Recent studies have shown that fatty liver disease, once associated mainly with alcoholics, is now alarming common, even in children, due to our high intake of sugar-laden foods and drinks.

So, eat lots of whole plants and whole grains and avoid the refined versions (white bread, white rice, white pasta) because they convert quickly down into the smaller glucose molecules when we digest them.

Over the past few decades our eating habits have moved away from whole foods towards processed and ultra-processed foods. Apart from the general negative health effects of those products (saturated fats, hidden sugar, preservatives, emulsifiers, even the dreaded trans fats etc) this shift has also resulted in the decline of our fibre intake. This over time has a dramatic effect on our gut health and our overall health. In recent years there has been a fibre revival, with a lot of experts communicating the message about the importance of boosting fibre intake. It also helps keep your poop activity regular.

Fibre is often listed on nutrition labels on foods but try and stay natural and eat whole plants. Many of the emerging factory made foods are now branding themselves as "plant-based" to align with health messaging. However, just because something is plant-based doesn't mean it's healthy and sometimes it's very hard to tell from the packaging and labelling unless you have a solid nutritional understanding. I prefer to tell people to simply eat lots more whole plants and whole grains and pulses. In 2022, I partnered with local farmers to create a '30 Diversity' box to make it much easier for me to hit this target. It arrives on my doorstep every week. I've been exploring how to make this available to other people to as many have been asking me for it. The logistics have been tough to navigate though. If I manage to figure it out it'll appear on our Neuron Wellness website so keep your eyes peeled (intentional veg pun haha).

- 23 -

Fluids

Drinking water is the habit I find the hardest. I don't really know why. I drink lots of decaffeinated coffee and kombuchas and green teas, but when it comes to plain old water I'm hopeless. I forget about it for hours and then when I remember I try and drink lots. If you're practicing intermittent fasting (or any fasting) water and teas/coffees in general are fine unless they're laden with milk and sugar. So, I tend to drink more in the morning because I'm not eating food then. Then throughout the afternoon my drinking slows up. I'm working on it.

Water is an essential part of our health. We can survive far longer without food than water because it contributes to multiple activities in the body including maintenance of body temperature and transportation of nutrients and waste. It also plays a role in your gut. Imagine the food (and your poop) as logs on the log flume ride at your favourite amusement park. Those logs whizz along the flume when the water is running. Once the water stops, they struggle to move and eventually come to a halt. It's important to keep everything moving throughout our gut intestine so staying well hydrated is important. I will try harder.

I'm also considering purchasing a reverse osmosis filter because the levels of "forever chemicals" that have been found in UK drinking water in 2022 is somewhat alarming. These chemicals are known to be harmful to health. Regular water filters don't remove these forever chemicals from tap water. These things are toxic and have been found to impact health even at lower levels than the national regulatory level. Depressing.

- 24 -

Field to Fork

Let's not dwell on this one as it's obvious and we've already mentioned it several times elsewhere.

We should be eating real food direct from its natural source. Not processed food made in factories.

We should choose organic where possible to avoid toxins from chemicals. This is especially true for the 'dirty dozen' list of fruits and vegetables I listed in the Neuron book and which is published by nutrition organisations each year.

The only interference should be the act of washing, preparing and cooking.

Any other messing around in factories by humans or machines is likely to be negatively impacting the nutritional value of that produce.

Buy fresh produce. Preferably local rather than global to help reduce the carbon footprint.

- 25 -

Fish & Feathers

The body is able to obtain many molecules necessary for health via plants. Our biology can also manufacture some chemicals itself. But omega fatty acids are polyunsaturated fatty acids that cannot be produced by us and are vital for many roles including acting as a major component of cell membranes throughout the body and brain. Hence, they are called the "essential fatty acids". They must be obtained via food sources.

A recent study found that low levels of omega-3 in your blood can shorten life expectancy more than smoking. That's a quite astonishing finding. According to the report, smoking knocked four years off life expectancy, whereas low levels of omega-3 reduced it by five.

Omega-3 is found in oily fish in abundance. Residents of 'Blue Zones" around the world, where people live the longest and are the healthiest (e.g. Okinawa, Japan / Sardinia, Italy), enjoy regular fish consumption. But how much oily fish do you eat each week? Is it enough? Some plants such as flaxseeds and walnuts also contain omega-3s but not in the way that fish do. If you're not a regular oily fish eater you might want to add a supplement to your routine.

The blue zone long-lived populations also did not eat much meat (only 2oz or less about 5x per month). A general "retreat from meat" is growing in popularity at the moment, partly driven by environmental concerns due to the pressure that animal rearing puts on crop and water supplies. But also for health reasons. The concern over the levels of saturated fat have been documented for many years. The links with high cholesterol (the bad type) and heart disease are known. Beef, pork and lamb are high in this type of fat. More recently, additional findings suggested the harmful effects of red meat could be due to a more complex combination of both the saturated fat and cholesterol response. Also a metabolite called TMAO that's produced when we digest red meat. These investigations are ongoing.

All in all, if you're going to eat meat it makes sense to veer away from red meat and stick with lean chicken. If you don't eat meat at all make sure you're getting sufficient protein from plant sources such as edamame, tofu, lentils, chickpeas, and almonds.

Animal welfare concerns are also contributing to this plant-based movement.

Force, Flexibility
& Fysicality*
(*forgive the F cheat)

In the 1990s, I originally qualified as a sport and exercise scientist majoring in psychology and physiology. I spent decades in this field and still work with elite performers today. Like my peers, I was utterly convinced that the fitness protocols we were promoting to the public would produce healthy nations.

They did not.

It's particularly concerning that these outdated methods are still being promoted to the public today as best practice.

Let's bust some myths here.

Of course, it's important to move our body. We need to do it frequently. I'm not advocating for a lack of movement. I'm calling for a reality check, so we stop giving people this default instruction telling them to join gyms and "get fit".

For millions of years, we've been activating our underlying biology constantly throughout our daily lives, even when at rest (remember the earlier chapter about furniture and the resting squat position).

The problem is that just as we've messed around with our natural food sources (inserting factories and machines) we've also messed around with our natural movement (inserting gyms and fitness machines).

I think it's essential to keep hammering home the message that there's a reason five decades of fitness failed to produce healthy nations. It's a highly inefficient approach that's based on flawed scientific methodologies. These protocols came out of elite sport. If you want to win a race or achieve a certain aesthetic physique then, yes, you need the gym and fitness protocols. But if you want to delay ageing, chronic illness, and death then you need wellness, not fitness. That means addressing some daily habits.

Let's unpack this a bit because I know some readers who are keen fitness fans are not going to want to believe it. I've infuriated many individuals at conferences I've spoken at. However, my point is that the fitness routines being given to most people are outdated and do not produce either the necessary cellular response, or fat burning response, or a habit that can be sustained practically and sustainably FOREVER. The forever part is crucial. That's why simple habits are key.

Here are a few points:

- Studies are showing that individuals who participate in frequent, extensive, intense exercise can actually experience accelerated biological ageing (believed to be due to an overtraining effect and the consequent low-level inflammation response caused by that excessive training load). I've witnessed this myself with clients I've worked with.

- If you're a busy executive working long days but proudly squeezing in your gym workouts 3 or 4 days a week after work, you're probably experiencing a negative wellness effect. This is because you're exposing yourself to bright lights, loud music, and the stress of having to travel to/from the gym, at a time of night where you should be winding your autonomic nervous system down ready for delta wave sleep, not hyperactivating and overstimulating it. Also getting home late results in eating late (too close to bedtime) and going to bed later – all those factors can result in impaired sleep quality and also negative blood glucose effects and eating choices the following day. Regular good quality sleep is a vital pillar of wellness.

- Studies of hunter-gatherer tribes are now suggesting we have a metabolic ceiling. In other words, burning extra calories on a treadmill now seems to just produce a biological compensatory effect, whereby other metabolic processes elsewhere (e.g. the immune system or cellular repair) are dialled down to require less calories to balance the books. Consequently, hunter-gatherers clocking up almost 20,000 steps every day, when compared with sedentary western office workers, didn't demonstrate as dramatic a difference in calorie expenditure as you might expect. You cannot "exercise off" your poor eating habits. It could result in negative long-term effects. Focus on fixing your actual eating habits.

There is no doubt that we need to move but I think the term "exercise" has become completely warped and misunderstood due to the way it's been communicated in relation to fitness over previous decades. Its Latin origins include references to simply "put into use", "make use of", "keep busy".

Yes, we need to move regularly but mostly we can just move slowly. Sometimes we can simply stand or squat. Exercise doesn't need to mean a gym workout, fitness class or sweaty activity that requires a special outfit. Just move more and engage your muscles. Get outdoors in daylight to trigger the true evolutionary environment and cellular responses.

Every now and then it's good to get out of breath (see previous pages about the Factors of Longevity and the cellular responses to adverse conditions)

We should try and engage a low-level hum of muscle activity as frequently as we can – by standing, kneeling or in a resting squat position.

We should slow the ageing-related decline of muscle tissue by exerting force regularly to encourage the development of new muscle cell growth. I use slow motion push-ups and climbing stairs two at a time to target this. I avoid lifts like the plague. Our muscle tissue plays an important role in multiple systems including metabolism and immune function.

We should maintain flexibility by regularly moving as our body design intended, through all ranges of motion from reaching up, lunging, twisting etc. Even small changes to your habits can help this movement happen naturally. For instance, I now lift my foot onto a high stool when tying my laces. This gives a great stretch of the hip flexors that tend to shorten due to modern sitting positions. This can lead to back pain. I put my favourite mugs on a higher shelf in my kitchen cupboard. I now draw my curtains from the top instead of waist height so I have to reach up at full stretch. Simple habits done every day produce accumulative benefits.

We should remember we are physical beings that are designed to move.

Get out of your chair, enjoy your physicality and appreciate it. Frequent movement delivers physical and mental health benefits.

My experience over decades makes me firmly believe we need to stop pushing people towards gyms and fitness classes and encourage better movement habits in daily routines. That is far more likely to be a sustainable practice.

- 27 -

Facts not Fake news

Oh boy, where do I start? We are living in an era of information overload. Most of it is a pile of crap but how do we tell which info is fact and which info is fake?

Back in the day we used to rely on trusted sources. I think this remains the only way to navigate the increasingly dubious streams of information we are bombarded with online. Health is big business. There are millions of companies who would all love to sell us a product. Social media has made the matter a million times worse because now these adverts land on our news feed and seem genuine. It takes time and effort to research them before deciding whether to trust and buy or not.

I've adopted a much simpler approach. I assume everything is potentially fake news unless from a highly credible academic or professional who I know is likely to be communicating real data. I know that if I'm reading it in a high-quality, peer reviewed, scientific journal it's credible. If it's been recommended to me by someone I consider a trusted expert source I believe it's credible. If it's something I've found online I always research it further before I decide whether it's accurate or not.

Sadly, many people are being hoodwinked into various diets, exercise plans and app subscriptions that all claim to deliver health benefits. This landscape is going to get more and more confusing as the lucrative longevity market continues to grow.

My advice is to choose professionals who you select to be your trusted source and sign up to their newsletters. Even then I would recommend checking what they say if possible – because everyone makes mistakes sometimes.

Accurate knowledge regarding the new science relating to health "dos and donts" seems to be the one essential ingredient almost everyone is lacking. It's vital we supplement it. When I started this Healthy Trilogy journey years ago, I pushed my academic ego to one side and questioned whether my knowledge was up to date. What I discovered when I dived deep into the latest longevity science shocked me. As an expert I was actually very out of date. So were (are) my peers. Writing this Health Trilogy book series has enabled me to research deeply in this field and has transformed the way I view wellness (and fitness) forever.

Get enthusiastic about learning. It's the best investment you'll ever make.

Another form of facts that I highly recommend is health data. We are living in the information era. There are lots of tech wearables, gadgets and biological tests that can give us an insight into the state of our internal health. I highly recommend that you try and build an interest in your biology and start measuring it. The simplest way to start is by using the bathroom scales to monitor your weight. Staying in control of your waistline is one of the biggest challenges of modern life. Quietly putting on just 1 pound per year can push you into obesity within a few decades. Resulting in a higher risk of chronic disease in your 50s, 60s, 70s, 80s. Those scales can give you invaluable data. I weigh myself a few times a week. If the weight is going up I extend my fasting period for a few days to bring it back down. It's simple.

Sleep trackers are also valuable tools because it's not just the length of our slumber time that's important, but also the quality of it. You have no idea of your sleep cycles and the level of slow wave deep sleep (delta brainwaves) and REM sleep unless you're measuring it. Essential repair and restoration processes take place during deep sleep. Important emotional and memory consolidation processes happen during REM sleep. High quality healthy sleep rotates through these sleep cycles several times per night. Start monitoring your sleep patterns so you can figure out what aspects of your daily habits are affecting it. I wrote about this in detail in my Neuron book.

Fitness trackers are also useful if you need a motivational tool but don't get too obsessed about your step count. Moving more regularly through the day appears to be more important than doing one extremely long walk and sitting down for the rest of the day. There are many studies debating the value of the "10,000 steps" target that has become an urban myth in terms of health goals. That number simply originated from a marketing campaign in Japan decades ago. It was not based on any scientific evidence.

I also measure my heart rate variability (HRV), which gives an insight into the state of my nervous system. High HRV indicates that the parasympathetic branch of your nervous system is dominant. That's a good thing. It suggests that you are experiencing low levels of chronic stress. A persistently low HRV on the other hand can indicate that the fight or fight arm of that system is overactivated. This can lead to chronic circulation of stress chemicals in your blood that over time can be damaging. Again, I explored this in much greater detail in my Neuron book.

One of the most exciting developments in health technology is the advances in biological testing. A growing range of tests are now available to consumers and are becoming increasingly affordable. Gut tests giving an insight into your gut function and diversity, inflammation tests giving an insight into your biological ageing rate, vitamin D tests, cortisol (stress hormone) tests and many others are now on the market.

It's never been easier to stay up-to-date with the facts about your current health status. This data helps you make decisions and habit adjustments in real-time, rather than being unaware of this underlying activity until it erupts as a late-stage chronic disease diagnosis years later. Remember, prevention is the key word and at the heart of my smart wellness habit plan.

- 28 -

Fun, Family, Friends & Fur

As I write this my furry, faithful friend is by my side as always. He's never far away. Dogs are very loyal companions and now that we've increasingly embraced them into our home environments, they've become an important member of the family. Cats too.

Studies suggest they also deliver more benefits than just company. Smiling, hugging, and stroking your beloved pet can also change your brain chemistry. When dogs and their humans gaze into each other's eyes the oxytocin levels in both parties can rise significantly. This is the bonding hormone seen between mothers and their babies. Oxytocin has a calming effect. We feel safe and loved through this attachment with another being. This can reduce feelings of fear, loneliness and anxiety and the underlying chronic release of the associated harmful stress chemicals.

Our friends and families deliver health benefits too. Humans are designed to be with other humans. Interaction and social contact give our brains an extensive workout as well as helping to boost positive brain chemicals.

We smile and laugh with friends and family. This helps promote a positive brain chemistry including neurochemicals such as dopamine and serotonin.

Having fun and being social is a hugely important part of health and is often overlooked. In recent years the NHS has begun to reinforce this message with the development of the Social Prescribing strategy. Music can also act as a superb social glue, bringing people together in singing, dancing, and live music performance settings.

Hanging out with the furry members of our family also bring other benefits. Recent studies have suggested that regular contact with animals can boost our gut health. This is because petting and stroking your animal can expose us to additional microbes it's picked up in the natural environment. There's some evidence that dogs contribute a higher level of different bacterial species to the home environment than cats.

When these studies came out the news headlines positioned pets as "the new probiotic". I don't think they can replace the health impact of the probiotic foods and drinks I listed earlier in this book. However, there seems no doubt your pets can deliver many different positive health benefits. Cherish them. They don't live as long as us. Although there's a fascinating dog ageing project in progress in the USA now. The aim is to understand how genes, lifestyle, and environment influence ageing for both dogs and their human owners. Ultimately, they hope to be able to extend dogs' healthy lives as well as humans.

- 29 -

Freedom, Finances & Focus

Psychological stress is very bad for us. The elevated stress chemicals our body produces when the fight, flight, freeze arm of our autonomic nervous system is activated can be seriously damaging. This sympathetic nervous system was not designed to be chronically engaged. It was designed to be used in adverse situations so we could respond as necessary to overcome fear and respond to climb bee-filled trees to retrieve honey, hunt wild animals for meat, run from predators or life-threatening rockfall. It's our emergency survival system that has enabled us to thrive and dominate the planet.

However, today that system is frequently activated by modern life stressors.

Feeling trapped in a job or relationship that makes you miserable results in chronic stress.

Feeling continuously worried about money results in chronic stress.

Financial wellbeing and employee wellness have both surged in recent years. The global pandemic fuelled this trend further. I now work with many leading corporate employers and SMEs, helping teach these smart wellness principles to their workforces.

Sometimes it's good to be totally honest with yourself. Many of us don't like change. It's far easier to plod along in the same job even if it doesn't align with your original dreams. Some of us don't feel we're capable of following our dreams. Some of us don't even talk about having dreams and ambitions because of fear of being ridiculed.

But what if we only have one life? Don't you want it to be the best life it could possibly be? Does that involve the need to make some changes? Probably.

What would help give you a feeling of freedom in both your work life and personal life?

What do you need to do to achieve financial security?

I highly recommend you ponder over these questions for a while, make a coffee, write some notes. Then formulate a plan. Once you have a plan you can start moving towards it with focused intent. You'll be amazed at what you can achieve when you focus on a plan. Stop selling yourself short. Remember the amazing pre-frontal cortex in the frontal lobe of our brain that we talked about at the start of this book. We have the in-built ability to solve problems, create solutions and act on them to achieve incredible results.

Chronic stress shortens your healthy life expectancy. Freedom lengthens it. Focus on emotional and financial freedom. We evolved in a vast beautiful landscape, not a confined stressful life. Think big and follow your dreams. Have a purpose to focus on. A sense of purpose has been shown to benefit health. It gives us a reason to exist. What's your purpose in life? Find something to get out of bed each morning and live your best life for.

30

Fear-Free (slow the F down)

If chronic stress shortens healthy lifespan, how do we eliminate it? It's possible to directly influence your autonomic nervous system and switch off our ancient fear/stress response.

Our breath can do it.

Our mindset can also do it.

Let me emphasise here that stress is not a bad thing. As we mentioned earlier those cellular pathways for longevity respond to adversity. So, a bit of regular stress is essential. Also, cortisol – the so-called stress hormone – is actually a core chemical that surges to create our morning wakefulness to draw us out of sleep. However, when stress is a constant, low-level, occurrence the opposite effect can result, increasing the risk of chronic disease.

Therefore, learning how to keep chronic stress at bay is a great asset when it comes to longevity. I detailed this in Neuron but will outline some key tips here.

The parasympathetic branch of your autonomic nervous system is responsible for rest, digest, and repair activity. When the sympathetic branch (fight or flight response) becomes dominant, the parasympathetic branch activity is dialled down.

For longevity purposes we should aim to occasionally trigger the sympathetic response using our adversity mimetics habits, but at other times we really want the parasympathetic branch to be dominantly activated. This reduces the accumulative damage of chronic stressful chemical secretion.

Here are three hacks to embed in your routine:

1. Breathwork

Slow your breath and extend your exhales. The vagus nerve of the parasympathetic nervous system is wired to our breathing, digestion and forms the gut-brain-axis. Breathing out for longer than you breath in activates the vagus nerve. This downregulates the sympathetic (fight or flight) system. Also embrace this breathing technique during your cold shower for added effect. Do this regularly to maintain a strong vagal tone and to keep this system calm and in control.

2. Mindset

Your thoughts create significant changes in your brain chemistry and the activation of your stress response. Thinking negatively, worrying and ruminating can become a habit that shortens your healthy lifespan. Embed a simple gratitude practice in your daily routine and whenever you catch yourself thinking negatively distract your thoughts elsewhere to break this habit. Gratitude is an easy way to boost positive brain chemicals and get the parasympathetic system activated. While having my morning coffee I simply list the good things in my life. "I'm happy and grateful for my good health and the good health of my family. I'm happy and grateful for this delicious coffee. I'm happy and grateful that I get to meet my friend for some fun today."

Sometimes I say the same things every day. It doesn't matter. All you're doing is drawing your mind to the positive things and away from the negative things and this increases the release of positive brain chemicals and decreases the release of stress chemicals.

3. Music

Our brainwaves synchronise to musical rhythms. This makes music a great metronome, enabling us to influence our thoughts, the release of brain chemicals, and the activation of brain networks. Listen to music that makes you feel strong, calm, invincible, fearless, confident, relaxed, happy. Different types of music will produce different emotions and feelings. Use whatever works for you. Slow music can also be a great tool to help slow down your breathing. Music is a supertool and one of my favourite biohacks as you probably already know if you're familiar with my work.

Live fear free, without worries sabotaging your brain and body, and with this ancient survival system calm and in control.

31

Fortissimo

Fortissimo is a music term indicating musicians to play very loudly by using more strength, force, and vigour. We should live like this, maintaining vitality and enjoying our time on this planet as much as we can.

Over the past 18 months I've been testing people's biological age using the GlycanAge finger prick test. People are frequently surprised at how bad their results are. The fittest people also can score badly as I've mentioned.

For my next project I'd love to test the biological ages of the world's leading music stars. It seems they defy ageing. On paper they should have aged very badly due to their decades long hedonistic lifestyles and exposure to ear splitting volumes.

But they're all still on stage and nailing their shows night after night. Bursting with force, vigour and vitality.

Paul McCartney, aged 80.

Ringo Starr, aged 82.

Mick Jagger, aged 78.

Keith Richards, aged 78.

Ronnie Wood, aged 75.

Robert Plant, aged 73.

Brian May, aged 74.

Roger Taylor, aged 72.
Nile Rodgers, aged 70.

Willie Nelson, aged 89.

Even Tony Bennett, in the grip of dementia performed a wonderful live show last year, aged 95.

It's not just the guys. The female music icons are still rocking out too.

Cher, aged 76.

Dolly Parton, aged 76.

Debbie Harry, aged 78.

Madonna, aged 63.

Stevie Nicks, aged 74.

Chrissie Hynde, aged 70.

Diana Ross, performed at Glastonbury 2022, aged 78.

These aren't just a few random longevity stars. I could have filled this entire book just listing well-known, and not so well-known, musicians who are still performing and touring aged 60s, 70s, 80s and 90s.

How is this possible? Their lifestyles surely should have impacted them by now.

Does music keep us young?

I think it definitely does keep us subjectively young (the age we "feel"). I've met quite a few rock stars aged 50+ and they continue to exude a youthful vibe. Diana Ross, aged 78, stopped in the midst of her Glastonbury gig to announce, "I feel 47!".

How old do you feel your subjective age is? Mine is at least twenty years younger than my chronological age and biological age. Even younger when I'm listening to music from my youth, and younger still if in a live performance setting (this was the basis of my PhD research).

Music definitely imparts a multitude of biological and psychological wellness effects. I won't go into them in detail here because I've already discussed this in my previous books. What I'm super interested in discovering now is whether music also keeps us biologically young.

If I can persuade these stars to literally lend me a hand so I can take a quick finger-prick blood sample, to measure their biological age, I'll find out the answer.

What can we learn from these examples in our daily lives?

Enjoy listening to loud music often and let it stimulate your nervous system via your ears and skin and produce "the chills".

Experience it with others to get even greater benefits from the social interaction.

Learn how to play it and perform it loudly too. Learning a musical instrument is proven to be one of the best ways of slowing cognitive decline and building new brain connections. This is precisely the highly complex, novel task to boost this positive effect known as neuroplasticity.

Wear ear protection because our hearing has probably already been battered through several decades of loud music already, so let's look after whatever hearing we have left.

The previous chapter outlined the importance of slowing down our autonomic nervous system, but sometimes it's healthy to rev it up too.

Conduct your days with force, vigour and vitality throughout life!

32

Frequency not Fixes

Since launching my smart wellness plan in 2020 I've watched thousands of people embark on it. There is one factor that determines whether it transforms their health (and life) or not. That factor is successful habit formation.

The programme teaches them the habits to adopt for longevity and the science that underpins those habits. They learn the reason the habits work and consequently build the desire to adopt them into their daily routine.

Some succeed, their health improves, and their healthy life expectancy increases.

Some fizzle out, revert to their existing habits and fail to create the new normal.

I've been fascinated by adherence and motivation my entire life. It's formed a core part of my work both as a practitioner and an academic. Some people are very naturally disciplined, but most are not.

I believe my greatest challenge now lies in communicating this smart wellness information in a way that increases the likelihood that people can successfully make the required habit adjustments. If we can crack that then we'll have a healthier nation full of centenarians who are still rocking out.

Your habits control your life. Approximately 40-50% of your daily actions are habits performed every day in almost identical situations. Your brain loves to automate actions and decisions because it reduces the amount of energy and processing power required. It's a smart and efficient tactic that's evolved over millions of years.

Are you a disciplined person who finds it relatively easy to break old habits and form new, better ones?

Or are you someone who has consistently tried to do that but always falls off the wagon?

Here's what I'd like you to do.

- Accept that some (possibly many) of your habits may seem inconsequential but they are causing cellular damage that is right now shortening your healthy lifespan and marching you silently towards a future diagnosis of a chronic disease.

- Agree to identify ONE habit and make a commitment to change it over the next 12-months. For most people this initial habit change should be focused on food behaviours because in our western lifestyle that's a leading cause of disease. Simply adopt a basic 16-hour fasting practice several days per week.

- The remaining pages of this book feature a 52-week habit tracker. Put this book somewhere prominent and start ticking off every day you manage to activate the habit (e.g. having a later breakfast to allow a 16-hour fasting period).

- Find other like-minded people who also want to embed this habit (or a different habit). Become habit buddies. It's much easier to succeed and hone your habits if you're not trying to do this alone.

We've been trying to find quick fixes for generations. That's what all the multi-billion-dollar diet and fitness fads were based on. The promise of fast, easy results. The truth of the matter is it doesn't work. Throwing yourself at quick fixes for a few months every year (usually in January when the annual guilt sets in) is not directly helping those cellular longevity pathways we talked about (AMPK, mTOR, sirtuins), and the chronic inflammation caused by cellular damage and low gut diversity, that accelerates cellular ageing.

Frequency is the key to success and longevity.

You need to make these smart wellness habits your new normal.

Forever.

I know you can do it.

Keep me updated on your progress.

10 HABITS FOR LONGEVITY – The New Normal

WAIT. Don't eat breakfast until 16 hours after you finished yesterday's dinner

CHILL. Turn your shower to cold before exiting, slow your breath and extend your exhales

SUNPOWER. Get those eyeballs outside asap so your brain gets the early natural daylight signal

SMILE. Say / think "I'm happy and grateful that..." (list some good things in your life)

BE HUMAN. Get some regular social exposure to people (friends, family or strangers)

LIVE BACTERIA. Enjoy a daily probiotic food or drink to boost gut microbe diversity

MOVE. Stand / walk a lot, use the stairs if you're able, get out of breath and stay strong

GUT DIVERSITY. Eat 30+ variety of plants per week (+ fish) & Vit D/K2 (&B12) sprays if needed

SLEEP. End 8-hour eating (& alcohol) 3-hours pre-bed and avoid screens and bright bulbs

BRAIN GYM. Engage in novel, complex learning tasks weekly (e.g. music tuition or language)

Smart Wellness® by

neuron™

This is my Top 10 Chart of habits. It's my "new normal" since I successfully embed the smart wellness habits in my daily routine in 2020.

- 33 -

Finale

So, there you have it. These pages mark the end of my Health Trilogy series. As I'm typing this, I feel quite emotional. These books have documented a personal journey I've been on for my own health as well as for general research and work purposes. I hope you've found it useful and have managed to adopt some of the insights and habits featured in these books.

I don't intend ever writing another book. It's a huge amount of work and commitment. I'd rather now focus on communicating these recommendations far and wide.

However, science moves fast.

In a few months (July 2022) the new James Webb space telescope will beam back the first images of deep space we've ever seen.

What will we find?

The samples currently being collected on Mars will also be analysed during this decade if they are successfully brought back to Earth in the next few years.

What will that reveal?

Was there life on Mars?

Did microbial life originate on Mars and accidentally reach Earth on one of the many asteroids that we know have landed here from Mars in the past?

Are we Martians if we originally evolved from those microbes billions of years ago?

Maybe we're not the only life form out there?

No-one has these answers. All these possibilities are now being openly considered by leading scientists around the world. We know a lot compared to our ancestors, but really, we still know very little.

We're living in an incredible era of advancement driven by sophisticated artificial intelligence and the ability to use machine learning to quickly make sense of huge volumes of data that would be impossible for humans to process. This is already opening new insights into our cellular activity.

Who knows what technological breakthroughs will happen in the coming years? Perhaps, science of the future may inspire me to write again one day.

For now, it's farewell from me. Thanks for your time and your interest.

Best wishes for a happy, healthy, long life.

Julia

PART THREE

Faster

Habit Tracker

I like to see fast results. I get impatient. But some things take time. You can't rush new habits. They need consistency over a prolonged period until they eventually become the new normal.

Putting a structure in place can help speed up the habit adjustment process because it helps reduce the likelihood of "forgetting" and slipping back into old habits.

Use these weekly log sheets to help quickly embed a solid fasting habit.

Once you've achieved that try and add some of the other smart wellness habits.

Don't try adopting them all at once. It's too much and will lead to failure.

Start with fasting by simply opening up a 16-hour period of no eating (e.g. have an earlier dinner and/or later breakfast to eat within and 8-hour window)

Then once you've nailed that in place as your new normal choose another habit to embed.

Then choose another one.

Etc.

Week 1	HABIT 1 e.g. (16-hour fast)	HABIT 2	HABIT 3	HABIT 4
Monday				
Tuesday				
Wednesday				
Thursday				
Friday				
Saturday				
Sunday				

Week 2	HABIT 1 e.g. (16-hour fast)	HABIT 2	HABIT 3	HABIT 4
Monday				
Tuesday				
Wednesday				
Thursday				
Friday				
Saturday				
Sunday				

Week 3	HABIT 1 e.g. (16-hour fast)	HABIT 2	HABIT 3	HABIT 4
Monday				
Tuesday				
Wednesday				
Thursday				
Friday				
Saturday				
Sunday				

Week 4	HABIT 1 e.g. (16-hour fast)	HABIT 2	HABIT 3	HABIT 4
Monday				
Tuesday				
Wednesday				
Thursday				
Friday				
Saturday				
Sunday				

Week 5	HABIT 1 e.g. (16-hour fast)	HABIT 2	HABIT 3	HABIT 4
Monday				
Tuesday				
Wednesday				
Thursday				
Friday				
Saturday				
Sunday				

Week 6	HABIT 1 e.g. (16-hour fast)	HABIT 2	HABIT 3	HABIT 4
Monday				
Tuesday				
Wednesday				
Thursday				
Friday				
Saturday				
Sunday				

Week 7	HABIT 1 e.g. (16-hour fast)	HABIT 2	HABIT 3	HABIT 4
Monday				
Tuesday				
Wednesday				
Thursday				
Friday				
Saturday				
Sunday				

Week 8	HABIT 1 e.g. (16-hour fast)	HABIT 2	HABIT 3	HABIT 4
Monday				
Tuesday				
Wednesday				
Thursday				
Friday				
Saturday				
Sunday				

Week 9	HABIT 1 e.g. (16-hour fast)	HABIT 2	HABIT 3	HABIT 4
Monday				
Tuesday				
Wednesday				
Thursday				
Friday				
Saturday				
Sunday				

Week 10	HABIT 1 e.g. (16-hour fast)	HABIT 2	HABIT 3	HABIT 4
Monday				
Tuesday				
Wednesday				
Thursday				
Friday				
Saturday				
Sunday				

Week 11	HABIT 1 e.g. (16-hour fast)	HABIT 2	HABIT 3	HABIT 4
Monday				
Tuesday				
Wednesday				
Thursday				
Friday				
Saturday				
Sunday				

Week 12	HABIT 1 e.g. (16-hour fast)	HABIT 2	HABIT 3	HABIT 4
Monday				
Tuesday				
Wednesday				
Thursday				
Friday				
Saturday				
Sunday				

Week 13	HABIT 1 e.g. (16-hour fast)	HABIT 2	HABIT 3	HABIT 4
Monday				
Tuesday				
Wednesday				
Thursday				
Friday				
Saturday				
Sunday				

Week 14	HABIT 1 e.g. (16-hour fast)	HABIT 2	HABIT 3	HABIT 4
Monday				
Tuesday				
Wednesday				
Thursday				
Friday				
Saturday				
Sunday				

Week 15	HABIT 1 e.g. (16-hour fast)	HABIT 2	HABIT 3	HABIT 4
Monday				
Tuesday				
Wednesday				
Thursday				
Friday				
Saturday				
Sunday				

Week 16	HABIT 1 e.g. (16-hour fast)	HABIT 2	HABIT 3	HABIT 4
Monday				
Tuesday				
Wednesday				
Thursday				
Friday				
Saturday				
Sunday				

Week 17	HABIT 1 e.g. (16-hour fast)	HABIT 2	HABIT 3	HABIT 4
Monday				
Tuesday				
Wednesday				
Thursday				
Friday				
Saturday				
Sunday				

Week 18	HABIT 1 e.g. (16-hour fast)	HABIT 2	HABIT 3	HABIT 4
Monday				
Tuesday				
Wednesday				
Thursday				
Friday				
Saturday				
Sunday				

Week 19	HABIT 1 e.g. (16-hour fast)	HABIT 2	HABIT 3	HABIT 4
Monday				
Tuesday				
Wednesday				
Thursday				
Friday				
Saturday				
Sunday				

Week 20	HABIT 1 e.g. (16-hour fast)	HABIT 2	HABIT 3	HABIT 4
Monday				
Tuesday				
Wednesday				
Thursday				
Friday				
Saturday				
Sunday				

Week 21	HABIT 1 e.g. (16-hour fast)	HABIT 2	HABIT 3	HABIT 4
Monday				
Tuesday				
Wednesday				
Thursday				
Friday				
Saturday				
Sunday				

Week 22	HABIT 1 e.g. (16-hour fast)	HABIT 2	HABIT 3	HABIT 4
Monday				
Tuesday				
Wednesday				
Thursday				
Friday				
Saturday				
Sunday				

Week 23	HABIT 1 e.g. (16-hour fast)	HABIT 2	HABIT 3	HABIT 4
Monday				
Tuesday				
Wednesday				
Thursday				
Friday				
Saturday				
Sunday				

Week 24	HABIT 1 e.g. (16-hour fast)	HABIT 2	HABIT 3	HABIT 4
Monday				
Tuesday				
Wednesday				
Thursday				
Friday				
Saturday				
Sunday				

Week 25	HABIT 1 e.g. (16-hour fast)	HABIT 2	HABIT 3	HABIT 4
Monday				
Tuesday				
Wednesday				
Thursday				
Friday				
Saturday				
Sunday				

Week 26	HABIT 1 e.g. (16-hour fast)	HABIT 2	HABIT 3	HABIT 4
Monday				
Tuesday				
Wednesday				
Thursday				
Friday				
Saturday				
Sunday				

Week 27	HABIT 1 e.g. (16-hour fast)	HABIT 2	HABIT 3	HABIT 4
Monday				
Tuesday				
Wednesday				
Thursday				
Friday				
Saturday				
Sunday				

Week 28	HABIT 1 e.g. (16-hour fast)	HABIT 2	HABIT 3	HABIT 4
Monday				
Tuesday				
Wednesday				
Thursday				
Friday				
Saturday				
Sunday				

Week 29	HABIT 1 e.g. (16-hour fast)	HABIT 2	HABIT 3	HABIT 4
Monday				
Tuesday				
Wednesday				
Thursday				
Friday				
Saturday				
Sunday				

Week 30	HABIT 1 e.g. (16-hour fast)	HABIT 2	HABIT 3	HABIT 4
Monday				
Tuesday				
Wednesday				
Thursday				
Friday				
Saturday				
Sunday				

Week 31	HABIT 1 e.g. (16-hour fast)	HABIT 2	HABIT 3	HABIT 4
Monday				
Tuesday				
Wednesday				
Thursday				
Friday				
Saturday				
Sunday				

Week 32	HABIT 1 e.g. (16-hour fast)	HABIT 2	HABIT 3	HABIT 4
Monday				
Tuesday				
Wednesday				
Thursday				
Friday				
Saturday				
Sunday				

Week 33	HABIT 1 e.g. (16-hour fast)	HABIT 2	HABIT 3	HABIT 4
Monday				
Tuesday				
Wednesday				
Thursday				
Friday				
Saturday				
Sunday				

Week 34	HABIT 1 e.g. (16-hour fast)	HABIT 2	HABIT 3	HABIT 4
Monday				
Tuesday				
Wednesday				
Thursday				
Friday				
Saturday				
Sunday				

Week 35	HABIT 1 e.g. (16-hour fast)	HABIT 2	HABIT 3	HABIT 4
Monday				
Tuesday				
Wednesday				
Thursday				
Friday				
Saturday				
Sunday				

Week 36	HABIT 1 e.g. (16-hour fast)	HABIT 2	HABIT 3	HABIT 4
Monday				
Tuesday				
Wednesday				
Thursday				
Friday				
Saturday				
Sunday				

Week 37	HABIT 1 e.g. (16-hour fast)	HABIT 2	HABIT 3	HABIT 4
Monday				
Tuesday				
Wednesday				
Thursday				
Friday				
Saturday				
Sunday				

Week 38	HABIT 1 e.g. (16-hour fast)	HABIT 2	HABIT 3	HABIT 4
Monday				
Tuesday				
Wednesday				
Thursday				
Friday				
Saturday				
Sunday				

Week 39	HABIT 1 e.g. (16-hour fast)	HABIT 2	HABIT 3	HABIT 4
Monday				
Tuesday				
Wednesday				
Thursday				
Friday				
Saturday				
Sunday				

Week 40	HABIT 1 e.g. (16-hour fast)	HABIT 2	HABIT 3	HABIT 4
Monday				
Tuesday				
Wednesday				
Thursday				
Friday				
Saturday				
Sunday				

Week 41	HABIT 1 e.g. (16-hour fast)	HABIT 2	HABIT 3	HABIT 4
Monday				
Tuesday				
Wednesday				
Thursday				
Friday				
Saturday				
Sunday				

Week 42	HABIT 1 e.g. (16-hour fast)	HABIT 2	HABIT 3	HABIT 4
Monday				
Tuesday				
Wednesday				
Thursday				
Friday				
Saturday				
Sunday				

Week 43	HABIT 1 e.g. (16-hour fast)	HABIT 2	HABIT 3	HABIT 4
Monday				
Tuesday				
Wednesday				
Thursday				
Friday				
Saturday				
Sunday				

Week 44	HABIT 1 e.g. (16-hour fast)	HABIT 2	HABIT 3	HABIT 4
Monday				
Tuesday				
Wednesday				
Thursday				
Friday				
Saturday				
Sunday				

Week 45	HABIT 1 e.g. (16-hour fast)	HABIT 2	HABIT 3	HABIT 4
Monday				
Tuesday				
Wednesday				
Thursday				
Friday				
Saturday				
Sunday				

Week 46	HABIT 1 e.g. (16-hour fast)	HABIT 2	HABIT 3	HABIT 4
Monday				
Tuesday				
Wednesday				
Thursday				
Friday				
Saturday				
Sunday				

Week 47	HABIT 1 e.g. (16-hour fast)	HABIT 2	HABIT 3	HABIT 4
Monday				
Tuesday				
Wednesday				
Thursday				
Friday				
Saturday				
Sunday				

Week 48	HABIT 1 e.g. (16-hour fast)	HABIT 2	HABIT 3	HABIT 4
Monday				
Tuesday				
Wednesday				
Thursday				
Friday				
Saturday				
Sunday				

Week 49	HABIT 1 e.g. (16-hour fast)	HABIT 2	HABIT 3	HABIT 4
Monday				
Tuesday				
Wednesday				
Thursday				
Friday				
Saturday				
Sunday				

Week 50	HABIT 1 e.g. (16-hour fast)	HABIT 2	HABIT 3	HABIT 4
Monday				
Tuesday				
Wednesday				
Thursday				
Friday				
Saturday				
Sunday				

Week 51	HABIT 1 e.g. (16-hour fast)	HABIT 2	HABIT 3	HABIT 4
Monday				
Tuesday				
Wednesday				
Thursday				
Friday				
Saturday				
Sunday				

Week 52	HABIT 1 e.g. (16-hour fast)	HABIT 2	HABIT 3	HABIT 4
Monday				
Tuesday				
Wednesday				
Thursday				
Friday				
Saturday				
Sunday				

REMEMBER

Your genes + lifestyle + environment dictate your longevity.

Our lives have consequences.

Daily habits are key.

Make them good.

SOURCE MATERIALS

The contents of this book have been inspired by the hundreds of expert interviews, University lectures, and podcasts I have consumed over the past 18 months.

If your interest has been ignited, and you'd like to explore additional deeper reading on the latest scientific insights, search your keyword of interest at these websites to ensure high quality facts:

pubmed.ncbi.nlm.nih.gov

nature.com

cell.com

My Neuron book also lists many great books at the end of every chapter.

THE HEALTH TRILOGY

By Dr Julia Jones

<u>Volume 1</u>
The Music Diet: A Rock & Roll Route to a Healthier, Longer Life, published in 2019.

<u>Volume 2</u>
Neuron: Smart Wellness Made Easy, published in 2021.

<u>Volume 3</u>
F-Bomb: Longevity Made Easy, published in 2022.